KEEPING YOUR

VALUABLE EMPLOYEES

KEEPING YOUR
VALUABLE
EMPLOYEES

Retention Strategies
for Your Organization's
Most Important Resource

SUZANNE DIBBLE

John Wiley & Sons, Inc.

New York • Chichester • Weinheim • Brisbane • Singapore • Toronto

Published by John Wiley & Sons, Inc.
Published simultaneously in Canada.

This publication is designed to provide accurate and authoritative information in regard to the subject matter covered. It is sold with the understanding that the publisher is not engaged in rendering professional services. If professional advice or other expert assistance is required, the services of a competent professional person should be sought.

Library of Congress Cataloging-in-Publication Data:

Dibble, Suzanne, 1939–
    Keeping your valuable employees : retention strategies for your organization's most important resource / Suzanne Dibble.
        p. cm.
    Includes index.
    ISBN 0-471-32053-6 (cloth : alk. paper)
    1. Employee retention. I. Title.
HF5549.5.R58D53   1999
658.3'14—dc21   99-20330

Printed in the United States of America.
10 9 8 7 6 5 4 3 2 1

To Estelle and Manny

Preface

There is a new, twenty-first century employment relationship. It is an updated version of the nineteenth century idea that employer and employee can negotiate the terms of work on an even footing. In actuality, at that earlier time the power was with the employer. An individual refusing to accept the terms of employment did not have a job. The new employment relationship gives employees at least as much power as employers.

This makes recruitment hard and retention even more difficult. An example:

You interview a promising candidate for a hard-to-fill position. She does well on the structured interview. She listens carefully and takes notes as you describe your company's very competitive salaries, outstanding benefits, and vast array of services. Then she asks:

"What will you do to retain me?"

You describe, again, your educational assistance program, commitment to 40 hours of training per employee per year, job posting system, and fitness center.

"Those are attractive. But I want to know how you recognize and reward accomplishments. You mentioned that employees have a lot of flexibility and I want to know how that actually works, not just what the policy states. And since I have a personal life, I want to know about the boundaries between work and the rest of my life."

In the new workplace you face the question of retention even before you make an offer.

The New Employment Contract

Welcome to the realities of the new employment contract. Companies today recognize that it is their people who can give them a competitive advantage. The business model at Sears links customer satisfaction to employee satisfaction to the bottom line. Other companies such as Microsoft know that they depend on the intellect and creativity of their workforce to stay ahead in fast-moving markets. They do everything they can to attract the best and the brightest. The implication is that attracting and retaining the right employees is more critical than ever.

Employees recognize that implication. They have been watching the downsizings and resizings. They have seen what happened to their parents and friends who relied on one employer for lifelong employment. They have felt the impact themselves.

Employees have learned that their career and personal success depends on their talents and how they develop and increase their skills. They are glad to see that companies are waking up to the value of having the right people at the right time. They know that they can achieve their goals by shrewdly bargaining for conditions that are best for themselves.

The *old employment contract* was built on a sense of mutual obligation.

Employee perspective: If I do a decent job I can keep my position. It's okay here and I am not looking around for another job.

Employer perspective: Employees like to work here and are not eager to go elsewhere. As long as I treat them okay I do not have to worry about retention. It takes care of itself.

That mutual obligation disappeared with downsizing, mergers, outsourcing, and all of the other events that have shaken the trust underpinning that relationship.

The *new employment contract* says:

Employee perspective: I cannot count on this company for my future employment, and even if I could I do not want to. I will stay if it is worth my while, but I will keep my eye on the market and be receptive to other opportunities.

Employer perspective: I need to attract and keep the people who will help me be successful. I cannot afford employees who do not contribute, especially the employees with the old "entitlement" perspective.

If you are responsible for staffing you may have seen this coming. You have read about the new trends in the labor market. Tom Peters analyzes the cutting edge; *Fortune* lists the best places to work. It all sounds exciting, challenging, and frustrating. How does this apply to your company? What must you do to attract and retain the people you need? How well are the methods you read about working for those companies? How well will they work for you?

Clearly we are in a time of transition. Some employees, and not just ones you recently hired, have the twenty-first century view of the employment relationship. They may be readers of *Fast Company*, the magazine that introduced the idea of "Free Agent Nation." Others, at any age, may have an entitlement mentality. Many are in between, struggling to understand and operate in the new workplace.

Meeting the Challenge

How do you meet the challenge of retaining the people you need when they come in such a great variety and have so many interests?

This book takes a systematic approach to help you figure out how to understand and respond to the new employment relationship. It is a how-to book. It gives you:

▶ A framework to determine how the new employment relationship applies to your situation.

▶ Techniques and tools for retention.

▶ Methods to determine what works for your organization.

This is a book for practitioners. It is for anyone who needs to know how to retain employees today. You are in the hot seat. You face unrelenting competition for the people who will make your company successful. It may be hard for your organization to design, implement, and sustain actions that support the new employment relationship. But the new employment relationship is here to stay. The challenge is great. This book will help you plot a course around the obstacles and make it possible for you to retain the employees you want to keep.

Acknowledgments

D iscussions with colleagues and coworkers over many years have provided insight into how organizations can retain employees. I want to thank Linda Henderson for her early interest and advice on the survey of employees in Chapter 18. Others who provided assistance for the book are: Jan Baietty, Sue Daniels, James Krolik, Rose Pelot, Sarah Preisinger, Susan Smith, Jan Twork, Susan Wainstock, and Joel Welsh.

I want to thank Lois Ann Hernquist, Cynthia Holste, Carl Dibble, and Ruth Dibble for critiquing the manuscript.

Most of all I want to thank my family, Ted, Ruth, and Miriam, and above all my husband Carl, who put up with my long hours and digressions.

This is my work and my words and my responsibility.

Contents

Contents *xv*

I

Why We Are Where We Are

1

Introduction

The difficulty that we have today in finding and keeping the skilled employees who make us successful is the result of a revolution. The revolution is our new understanding of the role of employees in our organizations. We now realize that those skilled employees make the difference between winning and losing. And, like other revolutions, its impact will be with us for a long time. If you think it is hard to retain employees now, be aware that in the future it will be worse.

The revolution in our thinking—that employees have a critical role in our success—led to the rise of the twenty-first century employment relationship.

▶ *Scarcity of skilled employees.* As more and more organizations understand that the right workforce gives them a competitive advantage, the demand for employees with the right skills increases. This is happening at all levels of the workforce, from frontline customer service representatives to professional engineering experts to top management. Employers

---

Retention Is Different from Turnover

As I write this in early 1999, the national unemployment rate is 4.3%. In Michigan, where I live, the rate has been hovering below 4%. It is convenient to attribute the difficulties in retaining employees to this low unemployment rate. The rate plays a role, but a small one. Employees who are unhappy, have a run-in with the boss, or are bored can quit and find another job. That shows up as turnover. Retention, on the other hand, is about keeping the skilled employees who make a difference. A higher unemployment rate may make it slightly easier to retain the employees we want to keep, but it will not change the fundamental difficulty.

---

need people with technical skills as well as analytic, communication, and other so-called soft skills; they need people who work creatively and deal effectively with customers. And they are finding that these people are in short supply.

▶ *Ability of employees to negotiate for their services.* If you have something to sell that is in short supply, then you can negotiate your price. That is the basic supply-and-demand philosophy in a market economy. It has always been present. In the past, a limited number of specialists and executives have been able to negotiate the terms of their employment. The difference is that now the market imbalance between the supply of and demand for labor appears in all types of jobs and at all levels of the organization. Now we see negotiations for bank tellers, computer programmers, and nurses. If you have skills that are in demand, then you have leverage with your current employer and opportunities to move to a different one.

The twenty-first century employment contract is the result. There has been a paradigm shift in the employee-employer relationship. The old contract was one of mutual obligation but an unequal power balance: It paired an employee's "doing a good job" with the employer's "I'll take care of you." The new contract is an exchange relationship in which each side has a degree of freedom.

The employee says: "I'll do my best as long as I can get what I need from you." In response, the employer says: "You'll have a job if you can contribute what I need as we go along."

The Impact of the Revolution Is Long-Term

This changes everything. The shift is not a temporary phenomenon. It is a result of long-term economic, political, and technological processes that have shifted power in the direction of the employee. Employees, especially the most capable ones, have an increased confidence in their ability to work under conditions that fill their own needs. They can negotiate the terms of employment that suit them and change jobs and careers to secure better conditions. The movement of power to the employee will continue over a long time, despite fluctuations associated with the economic cycle and specific labor markets. That is why retention is so important today and why we will continue to find it difficult to retain the employees we want to keep.

Overview of the Topics

This book looks at the key issues of managing human resources through the lens of retention. It starts from the premise that you have management or functional responsibilities for people and you want to improve your ability to retain the ones you want to keep. It assumes that you want practical information about different techniques that affect retention. It also assumes that you understand that your work environment is different from others. You cannot apply what you read without considering your unique environment. Throughout, the book looks at environmental factors that affect what we do. Perhaps most importantly it looks at what we do through the eyes of our employees. They are our customers and we need their perspectives.

We begin with a discussion of the employment relationship. It examines the trends that have caused the change in the workforce. We need to understand what created the new environment before we try to work within it.

From the perspective of the new relationship we move to an overview of staffing, getting employees we want for our organizations. Then we look at methods of managing retention. The tools may be familiar but the perspective is not. We look at what makes them effective in retaining employees and the necessary conditions for their use. There is a chapter on counteroffers, a rethinking of their use in light of the twenty-first century employment contract.

Now we move from the general to the specific: how to become an employer of choice. Employers of choice understand their own strengths, and their weaknesses, in attracting and retaining employees. The book closes with additional resources including a summary of my research on factors influencing employees to stay with or leave their employers. My purpose in this book is to highlight the actions you can take to retain employees. The emphasis is on the practical—what you can do now. Retaining the employees you want to keep is difficult but absolutely critical if your organization is to reach its goals. Here you will find the tools to do it.

2

Who Tore Up the Old Contract?

The old contract was based on assumptions of stable relationships and trust. It is the image of the 1950s. The image showed America as strong and confident. The American economy was insulated from the world economy. Husbands worked and wives stayed home to mind the children. High school students' main concern was whom to take to the senior prom. Work was work but you could look forward to a nice pension. There was peace and prosperity for all.

The world was not entirely like that, though. There were threats to our security. Not everyone shared in the prosperity. The family was not *Ozzie and Harriet*. The color of your skin or ethnic background made a difference. But for some Americans these were truly the good times. Jobs were plentiful, home ownership was possible, and automobiles with the freedom of movement they offered were attainable. For many, this postwar world produced an economic stability they had never known. Our nostalgic idea of the old contract was born there.

What were the conditions of the old contract?

► Employers or distant shareholders owned the business; there were no 401(k) or stock ownership plans to distribute stock to employees.

► Employers set the terms of employment in their own firms; if employees did not like it they did not have to work there.

► Employers had an interest in treating employees well; it provided them with a reliable source of workers who were capable of doing the work.

► Unions negotiated increases in pay, additional benefits, and better working conditions, which then improved pay, benefits, and working conditions for nonunion employees as well.

► Employees changed jobs early in their working life and then settled in with an employer, expecting to work there until they retired with a gold watch.

The relationship between employer and employee was paternalistic. The employer provided the work and the pay. The employer might provide extras such as a Christmas bonus, a summer picnic, or a helping hand if the employee suffered a personal tragedy. Employees in return were asked to follow the rules and do a good day's work for a good day's pay. If they did that, they would have a job for their working life and then a good retirement.

This description is oversimplified, of course. However, both employer and employees used this model as the basis of their employment relationship.

Then a new model emerged. It has not totally replaced the old one: That takes years and years. But the new model has become powerful. It gives us a new basis for the employment relationship. It does not apply to everyone, just as the old contract did not. Just like the old contract, it does shape the assumptions of both employer and employee. This is the twenty-first century employment relationship. We will take a look at it in the next chapter. Let us first examine the sources of the old model and the forces that tore it up.

Where the Old Contract Still Exists

For some employers and employees this contract is still real. An incident that epitomizes the old contract occurred in late 1995 at Malden Mills Industries, Inc., the producer of Polartec and other pile fabrics. When the factory in Lawrence, Massachusetts, burned down, the owner, Aaron Feuerstein, committed to rebuild the factory at the same location and paid out $15 million in wages to factory workers while they were not working. He was praised by many for his loyalty to his workers and considered an idiot by others who thought he should take the insurance money and run. Another way of looking at this was expressed by Thomas Teal in his article "Not a Fool, Not a Saint" in the November 11, 1996, issue of *Fortune*. What Feuerstein did, wrote Teal, was "to treat a work force as if it was an asset, to cultivate the loyalty of employees who hold the key to recovery and success, to take risks for the sake of a large future income stream."

Where Did the Old Contract Come From?

The old contract, the model that some of us remember from the 1950s, had its roots in the Middle Ages. Lords swore loyalty (fealty) to their king in exchange for his protection, and the serfs did the same to the lords. The person in the higher rank protected the person in the lower rank. The latter was expected to follow orders in exchange for protection from the uncertainties of life.

When we look at the 1950s employment relationship we see how this earlier idea appeared in the form of two words: loyalty and entitlement.

- ► *Loyalty.* Employees remain with their employer and do a good day's work.
- ► *Entitlement.* Employers are expected to take care of employees and provide a good day's pay.

The Beginning of the End

The industrial revolution led to a breakdown in those relationships. The history of the seventeenth through twentieth centuries is full of examples of employers having no obligation to workers: bad working conditions, use of child labor, cheating employees out of their pay, exploitation of women, exclusion of minorities. Employees, now on their own, began to form unions to redress the loss of a mutual relationship.

The old, medieval relationship had a moral basis. The basis of the emerging relationship between employer and employee was a legal one. Unions sought contracts that coupled their members' obligation to provide labor with the employers' obligation to provide decent pay, benefits, and working conditions. Unions and others concerned about the breakdown in the old order worked to enact legislation to protect workers.

The prosperity of the 1950s masked the strengthening of the second trend. It was easier for employers to be generous when they were doing well.

The World Changes

New forces began to emerge in the 1960s to push us further along in the direction of contractual bases for the employer-employee relationship and away from the moral ones. Those forces changed the competitive climate for organizations and forced them to reconsider the role of employees in their ability to achieve success. Two of the most prominent were:

- ▶ Technology—changing the pace of what we do and when and where we do it.
- ▶ Globalization—bringing new competitors for markets and resources.

At the same time the composition of the workforce was changing. More women and minorities entered the workforce. With them came new strains on the old management style. Women, especially those with young children, were struggling to balance the

---

A Short List of Events Affecting the Environment of Organizations

▶ Vietnam War.
▶ Steep increase in oil prices in the early 1970s.
▶ Breakup of the Soviet Union and the end of the cold war.
▶ Japanese success in consumer products from cars to VCRs.
▶ North American Free Trade Agreement (NAFTA).
▶ Computer chips with continual increases in power and decreases in cost.
▶ Deregulation in airlines, utilities, banking.
▶ E-mail and the Internet for information, communication, and commerce.
▶ Emergence of the European Economic Community as a global competitor.
▶ Growth of Chinese influence in the world economy.

---

claims of work and family. They asked for and then began to insist on accommodations at work. Minorities, hardly a monolithic group, challenged the way they were viewed. They asked to be treated according to the skills they brought to the workplace and not on stereotypical perceptions of their ethnicity.

Organizations were challenged both from the outside by technology and globalization and from the inside by the demands of the changing workforce. Books and articles in the business and academic presses dealt with how and why the United States lost its competitive powers. A literary genre grew up around the idea that the United States could not compete in world markets and was being beaten at home. Managers began to realize that to compete in this new environment they had to be flexible, nimble, and fast reacting. The accustomed way of operating had to change. Something had to give way.

Organizations Struggle to Compete

The reality was far more complex than the preceding description. Not every organization was affected in the same way or reacted in the same way. Some organizations responded by reconsidering what they were in business to do. Mission-driven nonprofits were less affected, but many governmental units participated in this reevaluation. Organizations redesigned themselves around their core and reengineered, downsized, realigned, and otherwise changed themselves.

As they were doing so, they pushed hard on the old contract. The elements of loyalty and entitlement, already under strain from new trends based on legal arrangements, were under enormous pressure. What happens when you push hard against a crumbling object? It breaks apart and the forces that had buffeted it from the other side emerge.

The outcome was that employees without skills to produce results for the core business were no longer valued. Work was outsourced. Employees lost jobs or accepted lesser positions with little future. This in itself was not new. Layoffs had occurred under the old contract. Even during the 1950s, when the old contract flourished for the last time, reorganizations or poor profits resulted in employees losing their jobs. Those actions did not greatly undermine trust. This time it was different.

Some Reasons Why Trust Disappeared

The forces undermining stability, trust, loyalty, and entitlement grew over a long period of time. Some of the contributing management actions are:

▶ Treating frontline employees—customer service representatives, bank tellers, repair technicians—as interchangeable.
▶ Giving large pay packages to executives while limiting other employees to small increases.
▶ Repeatedly trying to change the culture with "programs of the month."
▶ Rewarding longevity, not ability or productivity, with money and promotions.
▶ Downsizing without regard to the impact on employees.

The Search for Skilled Employees

While organizations were reinventing themselves they reconsidered the role of people. To be competitive, to be flexible, nimble, and fast reacting, required employees with the right skills. The technical skills to outengineer, outmarket, and outthink the competition were critical. Equally important were such skills as planning, initiative, creativity, customer service, and risk taking.

To move quickly you have to cut down on the time it takes to make decisions. If you want employees to make decisions they need to:

▶ Know and understand the business and its objectives.

▶ Have information to make good decisions.

The need for talented employees occurred at the same time that terms of the old contract—stability and trust—were disappearing. The new contract broke through. The next chapter describes its terms.

▶ *To Go Further*

Gubman, *The Talent Solution.*
Hamel and Prahalad, *Competing for the Future.*
Judy and D'Amico, *Workforce 2020.*
Peters and Waterman, *In Search of Excellence.*
Ulrich and Lake, *Organizational Capability.*

See the Bibliography for citations.

3

The New Contract

The new contract is based on an exchange. When you can no longer rely on trust, you need something more specific as a basis for a relationship. One thing you can do is to have something that the other party wants and is willing to pay for. (As we will see in Part III, "Managing Retention," payment is not necessarily made with money.)

The new contract has its own conditions:

▶ Employees may have an ownership stake in the business; 401(k) and stock ownership plans make this possible, although the same management still runs it.

▶ Employers establish a structure for the terms of employment and employees can negotiate their own terms within this structure.

▶ Employers continue to have an interest in treating employees well (it is the only way to have a chance to retain employees with the right skills).

Why Do Employees Quit Their Jobs?

One answer appeared in the headline of a February 1, 1998, article in the business section of the *New York Times:* "Why Do People Quit Their Jobs? Because They Can." Another appeared on the cover of the December–January 1998 edition of *Fast Company* magazine: "Free Agent Nation." Inside, the Letters from the Editors described the members of this nation as having "written a new bill of rights for business: Freedom is security. Work is fun. Working solo isn't working alone. You are what you do."

▶ Unions negotiate pay, benefits, and working conditions but it is not always for improvements in pay and benefits; and the impact of unions has diminished, as their membership is a declining percentage of the workforce.

▶ Employees change jobs early in their working life and continue to change jobs, which may include working for themselves.

When the contract is no longer worthwhile for one or the other party, it will begin to dissolve. Employees who find that they are no longer getting what they want from their current job will look for alternatives, within or outside their current employer. Employers who decide that an employee no longer has the right skills have options. If the employee's skill is not adequate there are performance improvement plans. If the skill is not longer useful, perhaps because the employer is getting out of a business, then layoffs are a result.

The new contract is spreading. Employees with confidence in their skills, and with skills that are in demand, are leading the way. The old contract still exists in many places, but it is on the way out. *The new contract is strongest among the employees we want most.* How to operate in it effectively is the topic for the rest of this book.

4

As We Go Forward

The two preceding chapters briefly sketched why we are where we are. As we move to the practical sphere and begin to act, there are three imperatives:

1. Identify employees we want to keep. Suppose we do not need to keep all of our current employees. How do we identify the ones to focus on?

2. Understand the cost of losing employees. The cost to replace any employee is high. What are those costs and what are the still higher costs of replacing the employees we want to keep?

3. Assign responsibility for action. We cannot increase our ability to retain employees without someone taking deliberate, thoughtful action. Who takes those steps and how do we decide who should?

Identify Employees We Want to Keep

Who are those employees we want to retain? They are the ones who have "talent" and are "contributors."
They are the employees who make a difference to our:

▶ Customers.

▶ Other employees.

▶ Shareholders/boards/constituents.

These employees demonstrate:

▶ Breadth as well as depth of technical/functional knowledge.

▶ Customer service.

▶ Creativity.

▶ Continuous learning.

▶ Flexibility.

▶ Self-direction.

▶ Commitment to the organization's success.

These valuable employees are not concentrated at the top of the organization. They are spread throughout, at the frontline, in the back room, and in leadership positions. They are customer service representatives, programmers, accountants, nurses, clerks, and program coordinators.

How Do We Know Who They Are?

The employees we want to keep differ from others with the same job title. They are known by their skills. They may be customer service representatives with good listening abilities who identify what the customer needs and then use good organizational skills to respond to those needs. They may be the administrative assistants who can adapt to multiple priorities, maintain good relations with a large staff, and continue to produce good results on time despite repeated interruptions.

We identify the people we wish to keep by our own behavior. For example:

> We have three senior analysts but everyone goes to Lydia. Her coworkers and customers know that she will consider their questions or requests with an open mind. Her suggestions will be responsive; furthermore, she will help the coworkers or customers think through the situation. Lydia's supervisor as well as other members of management go to Lydia for information. Lydia is the one that everyone wants on projects because she will contribute in meetings and follow through afterward. Lydia is valuable for her knowledge as well as the way she communicates with others.

Lydia works with internal customers and is herself a customer of other employees. It is a little harder to identify the employees we wish to keep when they have primarily external relationships. We need to learn how their external customers or suppliers act toward them. We can collect compliments and complaints and, if necessary, survey the external contacts. If Sam is their contact with our organization, we want to know how Sam treats them. Would they continue to work with Sam if they had a choice? What is it that Sam does that makes him a good, or not so good, representative of our organization?

How Many Employees Do We Want to Keep?

Knowing the scope of a problem tells us its degree of urgency. We do not know the actual number of employees we want to retain in our organization. A working assumption is that the employee population follows a normal distribution:

▶ Crucial to our success and we want to do everything we can to keep them: 3%.

▶ Very important and we are willing to do a lot to keep them: 13%.

Figure 4.1   Distribution of the employee population.

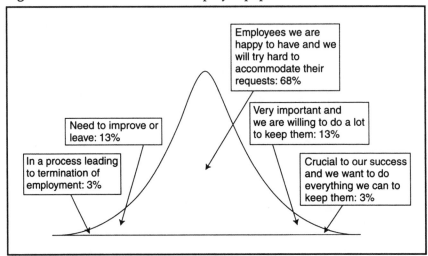

▶ Employees we are happy to have and whose requests we will try hard to accommodate: 68%.

▶ Need to improve or leave: 13%.

▶ In a process leading to their termination of employment: 3%.

Figure 4.1 depicts the normal distribution.

Quantify the Cost of Losing Employees

Consider a typical day:

▶ Craig, a key project manager, leaves for a position with a competitor. He will be doing similar work and earning $10,000 more than you pay him. Craig's supervisor comes to you and asks, "Why didn't you let me give Craig more money? It will cost me a lot more than $10,000 to find and train his replacement."

▶ Janice, one of your top tellers, says that she is resigning and going to work at another bank. She will earn 55 cents an hour more than she gets from you. In addition, she is excited by the opportunity to move into a management training program. Her supervisor says, "We will really miss her. I know that I couldn't give her more in wages, but isn't there anything that I could do to keep her? She is my senior teller. Could we have a new grade to reward someone of her experience and competence?"

How much does it cost to replace Craig or Janice? We know that it costs a lot to replace a good employee, but how much? We cannot put a hard number on it unless we have data on costs, and we may not have a model that identifies the costs we need to examine. We rely on our accounting and budgeting systems for information on operations, but those systems are not designed to identify costs associated with performance and productivity. We know how much we spend on advertising but not on overall recruiting. We can look up the amount we spend on external training and development but not the cost for internal training. We know our healthcare costs but not their benefit in attracting, motivating, and retaining employees. We have financial models for the replacement costs of our nonhuman resources but not our human ones.

Organizational decisions are often made on the basis of cost and other hard data. When we do not have data, we have difficulty ad-

---

It Is Hard to Make a Case without Having the Numbers

Suppose you had anticipated that Craig might leave and had gone to your boss to ask for more money for him. What would you say about the cost to the organization if Craig were to leave versus giving him a $10,000 increase? What justification would your boss look for? Every organization answers this differently. What would yours say today? Has this answer changed over time?

vocating a position. In some organizations, when there is no cost data the cost is treated as if it is zero.

We would like to support Craig's and Janice's supervisors. We would like to make the case that there are costs to losing employees. If we knew the costs we could do something differently. Although it might be too late to affect Craig or Janice, we could make changes that would prevent the loss of talented employees in the future.

A Model for Costs

The worksheet in Figure 4.2 is a model for beginning to estimate the costs associated with not retaining employees. It identifies the factors that go into attracting, motivating, and developing employees. It looks at the productivity of employees and the costs associated with an employee's leaving the organization. The work sheet has five categories:

1. Separating an employee from the organization.
2. Hiring a new employee.
3. Developing a new employee to the level of the employee replaced.
4. Losses between the time the old employee leaves and the new becomes equally productive.
5. Loss of the potential future contribution of an exceptional employee.

Use estimates when there is no data. A series of estimates gives a better idea of the cost of replacing an employee than one big guess.

▶ *To Go Further*

Cascio, *Costing Human Resources.*

See the Bibliography for citation.

Figure 4.2 Cost of replacing an employee.

(Consider labor and nonlabor dollars for human resources, the hiring department, and other functions with responsibilities.)

ACTIVITY   DOLLARS

Separating an employee from the organization

▶ Exit interview—employee and interviewer time.   _____

▶ Good-bye party on work time.   _____

▶ Administrative—take employee off the payroll, process final pay, COBRA, transfer out of retirement and other plans, prepare and send communications.   _____

▶ Overhead.   _____

    Subtotal for separating an employee.   _____

Hiring a new employee

▶ Job description—verify that the position should be filled, review description, and revise if necessary.   _____

▶ Recruitment—post jobs, design advertising, place ads, identify where to recruit and make contact, appear at job fairs/conferences/campus recruiting sessions, process resumes, track and maintain resumes and applications, prepare and send communications.   _____

▶ Selection—screen resumes, provide information to potential employees, schedule interviews, bring in potential employees for interviews and tests, interview, test, reach consensus, check references, negotiate offer, pay referral or hiring bonus or both, do physical exam (post-offer), relocate, prepare and send communications.   _____

▶ Orientation—provide information and documents, enroll in benefits and other services, orient to organization, orient to work unit, prepare and send communications.   _____

(Continued)

Figure 4.2 *(Continued)*

▶ Administration—track activities to fill the position, add employee to payroll, benefits, and services. _____

▶ Provide necessary equipment. _____

▶ Overhead. _____

Subtotal for hiring an employee. _____

Developing a new employee to the level of the employee replaced

▶ Training—classroom training (internal and external), on-the-job training. _____

▶ Development—coaching, mentoring, testing. _____

▶ Overhead. _____

Subtotal for development. _____

Losses between the time the old employee leaves and the new is as productive

▶ Lost business due to missing products or services. _____

▶ Increased costs due to lower skills. _____

▶ Poor morale. _____

▶ Overtime pay. _____

▶ Pay for temporary workers. _____

▶ Overhead. _____

Subtotal for losses. _____

Loss of the potential future contribution of an exceptional employee

▶ Value of contribution. _____

Offset

▶ Labor savings from open position. _____

What is the bottom line? _____

Know Who Is Responsible for Retention

Who has this responsibility in your organization?

- ▶ The supervisor?
- ▶ Second-level supervision?
- ▶ The human resources (HR) department?
- ▶ Senior management?

The answer is all of them.

- ▶ Craig's supervisor wanted to give Craig a developmental opportunity but needed approval from his supervisor for funds for external training. The supervisor's boss is sitting on the request because he is over budget now and is waiting until next quarter when he will have more flexibility.
- ▶ Janice's supervisor had not considered the possibility of a management training program as a retention tool until Janice was about to leave. Dan in human resources does compensation surveys and noticed that other banks were adding management training programs. He planned to discuss it with Janice's supervisor but first wanted to put it in proposal format.
- ▶ Senior management talks about retention but takes months to approve a flextime plan. They see the logic of it but want to know its impact on costs and on retention. Will it disrupt operations to have employees start and stop at different times? What is the impact on productivity? Will it actually retain employees?
- ▶ Meanwhile, human resources does not have time to analyze exit interview data because the staff is working on the implementation of a new human resources information system.

The danger of a shared responsibility is that none of the parties really takes responsibility. No one is quite sure of his or her own role and what he or she must do. To effectively accomplish an objective such as retaining the employees we want to keep, we have to find a way of clarifying and meshing the individual responsibilities.

Suppose you were appointed the "retention czar." You are told that retention of employees critical to your organization's success is your top priority and that your future in the organization depends on your ability to retain those employees. You would start by identifying everyone who has a role in retention and work with

Who	Responsibility
Supervisors	▶ Identify the employees.
	▶ Learn what it will take to retain them.
	▶ Plan and take actions based on what it takes to retain the targeted employees.
	▶ Suggest other steps that will retain the targeted employees.
	▶ Identify barriers to doing what you need to do to retain the targeted employees.
Second-level supervision	▶ Provide the resources needed by the first-level supervisor.
	▶ Monitor progress.
	▶ Suggest other steps that will retain the targeted employees.
Human resources	▶ Develop and train supervisors to lead and coach.
	▶ Design and develop programs that improve the quality of work life.
	▶ Survey employees to identify areas in the work environment that need improvement.
	▶ Monitor exit interviews and alert management to issues.
Senior management	▶ Maintain an open-door policy.
	▶ Support recommendations of supervisors and human resources or tell them why not, quickly.

them to assign clear individual responsibilities. This includes defining the role of senior management. See box for one possible result.

Retention is a serious and ongoing issue. It is a problem that we will continue to face for the foreseeable future. The employees we want to retain are always in short supply and always have alternatives. As you develop your own plans and programs to increase your ability to retain the employees you want to keep, the three factors of identifying who you want to keep, quantifying costs, and assigning responsibility, will help you focus on the essentials.

II

Foundations of Retention

5 | Retention Starts with . . . Job Descriptions, Recruitment, Selection, Orientation

Retention begins long before an employee's first day on the job. It starts when we describe the position we plan to fill. It is at stake when a potential employee, someone with the skills we need, reads our ads or talks with a recruiter. Retention is affected when we interview her and give her a chance to interview us. Retention also starts when she accepts our offer and begins the process of becoming our employee. Everything we do before her first days of work impacts our ability to retain her once she is here.

Job descriptions, recruitment, selection, and orientation are the foundations of retention. More than ever, doing them well is critical.

We know already what happens when they are not done well.

▶ If the job description does not define what we are looking for, we do not recruit people with the skills we require.

▶ If recruitment efforts reach a limited number of potential employees, we do not have enough good people to choose from.

▶ If our selection process does not focus on the competencies we have defined, we will not have the person who meets the requirements of the position.

▶ If orientation does not begin to engage employees in our organization, they are not going to contribute to our goals.

Both the organization and the employee are beginning a relationship that will not last if there is a mismatch between the position requirements and the new hire's skills. It makes no difference if the mismatch is due to our not knowing what we need, not having the right person in our candidate pool, not selecting the person who can do the work, or not launching the person we hire on the right track. The results are, on either side, unfruitful.

▶ For the organization: loss of productivity because work is not getting done or not getting done right; burnout of overworked employees; the often hidden cost of management time to fix the problem.

▶ For the employee: frustration due to not being able to use one's skills; investment of time and energy to find another position.

Laying the Foundation

In the twenty-first century employment world we must look at the foundations of retention through the eyes of potential employees. They are the customers for our jobs. If we do not prepare a good foundation, we cannot expect them to stay. Employees will no longer endure what they do not like in their employment situation. They have power in the knowledge of their abilities and confidence in their value in the marketplace. With greater loyalty to their career and their skills than to their employer, they move on.

The twenty-first century employment relationship puts enormous pressure on organizations to lay a solid foundation for the employment relationship. The next four chapters describe how to

> ### *We Are Better Off under the New Employment Relationship*
>
> In the old employment relationship, we as employers often felt that it was up to us to fix the situation. We were faced with unpleasant alternatives:
>
> ▶ Fire mismatched employees.
> ▶ Move them out of their jobs into something else.
> ▶ Train them to develop the skills required.
> ▶ Change what we require to match what they can do.
>
> In the new employment relationship we do not always have to solve the problem of a bad hiring decision. Often the employee knows that he or she made a bad decision in agreeing to the offer and will look for another job.
>
> Although the now ex-employee has relieved us of the need to take action, we are still stuck. We have invested our resources in trying to fill a position and now we have to do it again.

build that foundation. We will examine job descriptions, recruitment, selection, and orientation, looking at each from both the employees' perspectives and our own.

These chapters assume you already know how to prepare job descriptions, recruit, select, and orient. Here the objective is to build on your knowledge of managing human resources and show how the actions you take affect your ability to retain the employees you want to keep.

6

Retention Starts with Job Descriptions

The first step in building a foundation for retention is have a clear picture of the work we want the employee to do and the skills required to do it. The written form of this clear picture is a job description. To support retention, job descriptions should do four things:

1. State the purpose of the job—why it exists in the organization.

2. Describe the basic responsibilities.

3. List the skills needed to perform the responsibilities.

4. Describe the working conditions.

Figure 6.1 is an example of a job description.

Figure 6.1   Job description as a foundation to retention.

Job Description

Title: **Administrative Assistant**   Grade/Level _____

Reports to: **Manager**   Exempt status _____

Department: **Customer Contact**   Date __/__/__

Basic Functions

Serves the external customers of XYZ Company by supporting the work of the customer contact representatives (CCRs) and their work environment; maintains inventories of supplies and material required by the staff to perform their tasks and to provide service to customers; posts schedules and availability lists so CCRs can plan for coverage; prepares and processes all nonroutine correspondence and communications including advertising material, statistical reports, scheduling, and personnel changes; coordinates communication among customers, suppliers, and staff regarding products and services.

General Duties and Responsibilities

1. Process invoices; open and receipt invoices; verify transactions and amounts; prepare for payment; assign accounting and post invoices to appropriate accounts; maintain files of invoices; verify payment reports.

2. Maintain an efficient level of supplies; set and/or observe reorder levels; learn lead time for orders and delivery schedules and place orders as necessary or as scheduled; receive supplies and maintain supply cabinet and storeroom; make supplies easily accessible to all staff.

3. Coordinate training for staff as identified in their development plans; maintain list of courses and availability; post training schedules and sign-up lists; coordinate external training including payments and travel; set up and coordinate training for new employees.

4. Prepare statistical reports for the department; run weekly and monthly reports using staff input; identify variances and

---

Figure 6.1   *(Continued)*

collect information to provide explanation; post results on the department bulletin board; forward results to management.

5. Prepare nonroutine correspondence and presentations; gather information on content and intended audience; work with principal to prepare work appropriate to occasion and audience.

6. Process personnel data changes; enter data; maintain confidential files; set up work space for new employees; act as an information resource on personnel policies and procedures for staff.

7. Take other actions to meet basic responsibilities of position.

Job Requirements

▶ Education: Two to three years of course work beyond high school in accounting, business, or related field or equivalent work experience.

▶ Work experience: Two or more years in providing administrative support to an operation.

▶ Skills (see below for definitions and behaviors):

Administrative skills.
Analysis/problem solving.
Attention to detail.
Communication.
Organization culture and knowledge.
Technical.

Physical Demands

While performing the duties of this job, the employee is frequently required to sit and talk or hear; use hands to finger, handle, or feel objects, tools, or controls; and reach with hands and arms. The employee is occasionally required to walk. The employee must occasionally lift and/or move up to 10 pounds. Specific vision abilities required by this job include close vision and the ability to adjust focus.

Working Conditions

Normal business hours.

(Continued)

Figure 6.1   *(Continued)*

Administrative Assistant Job Description: Skills and Behaviors

Administrative Skills   Performing everyday tasks in an organized and efficient manner; managing time and information to ensure that information flows appropriately and that priorities are met.

1. Examines procedures to identify aspects that can be improved.
2. Applies policies and procedures that affect the job.
3. Understands how the work of other departments affects one's own work.
4. Obtains the resources needed to do own job.
5. Sets priorities for one's own work.
6. Prepares concise, informative, and timely reports for others.
7. Organizes materials within own work area.
8. Identifies resources to perform work when not available.
9. Prepares descriptions of key tasks so that others may perform them.
10. Develops a method of sharing information with others.

Analysis/Problem Solving   Securing relevant information and identifying key issues and relationships from a base of information; relating and comparing data from different sources; identifying cause-effect relationships.

1. Identifies issues requiring decisions.
2. Establishes clear criteria for decision making.
3. Understands assumptions underlying issues, and questions them.
4. Collects necessary data before making decision.
5. Identifies trends in data or activities.
6. Identifies small irregularities and prevents larger problems.
7. Uses mathematical techniques to analyze data.
8. Uses computer-based techniques to analyze data.

Attention to Detail   Accomplishing tasks through concern for all aspects involved, no matter how small; showing concern

---

Figure 6.1 *(Continued)*

---

for all aspects of the task; accurately checking processes and tasks.

1. Establishes a systematic method of tracking work.
2. Contacts vendors to verify that expected supplies will arrive as scheduled.
3. Follows up with clients and customers after handling problem.
4. Reconfirms meetings, reservations, and other arrangements.
5. Contacts customers or clients to determine the satisfaction with service.
6. Follows up on contacts to ensure that message is clear.
7. Understands dependencies across tasks.
8. Sends reminders on meeting content and arrangements.
9. Advises others of the potential impact of their delays on one's own work.

Communication Expressing ideas effectively in individual and group situations and in writing, including adjusting language or terminology to the characteristics and needs of the audience; supporting message with appropriate nonverbal actions and listening; using appropriate structure, grammar, and spelling.

1. Asks other staff members questions to clarify information.
2. Avoids gestures that distract from words.
3. Paraphrases the words of others to show understanding.
4. Demonstrates complete attention and clear understanding of issues.
5. Does not ramble.
6. Maintains eye contact.
7. Provides clear direction, orally, to others who depend on the information.
8. Summarizes key points.
9. Expresses ideas and facts in a concise, clear, and logical manner.
10. Adjusts language to a variety of audiences.
11. Provides clear written direction to others.

(Continued)

Figure 6.1   *(Continued)*

Organization Culture and Knowledge   Understanding how the company is organized and administered and how it relates to other organizations, customer groups, industry groups, and governmental units; perceiving the impact of actions taken on all parts of the organization; perceiving the impact of actions on customers and suppliers.

1. Understands goals statements and business objectives.
2. Applies quality tools to work processes.
3. Knows which regulations affect the work of the department.
4. Acts safely on the job.
5. Maintains current knowledge of organization's products and services.
6. Respects diversity in the workplace.
7. Makes suggestions to improve products and services.
8. Is committed to personal development.

Technical/Professional Knowledge   Successfully completing training in the appropriate subject matter and applying that knowledge in the workplace; keeping current with the subject matter and trends in area of expertise.

1. Maintains data on a computerized database.
2. Applies knowledge of economic reorder quantities to maintain material and supplies.
3. Explains budget variances to others.
4. Knows the limits of own technical expertise.
5. Uses computerized text tools to enhance communications.
6. Coaches other staff members on computer equipment.
7. Knows the personnel database systems, including data elements and timing of operations.
8. Uses the customer database to obtain information to support operations.
9. Accomplishes appropriately complex tasks without asking for instruction.

Support for the Foundations of Retention

A well-designed job description supports the other foundations of retention.

During *recruitment* a job description:

▶ Gives language for job postings, advertisements, executive recruiters, and job fairs.

▶ Serves as a basis for creative thinking on where to find non-traditional potential employees.

During *selection* a job description:

▶ Identifies the competencies and behaviors to use for interviews and other tests.

▶ Tells what we need for a job simulation and other content tests.

▶ Structures interview questions and probes.

▶ Provides a basis for assessment centers.

▶ Lists the required licenses and certificates we screen for.

▶ Suggests whom (coworkers, customers, or suppliers) to include in interviews.

During *orientation* a job description:

▶ Identifies job-specific resources that we need to have ready for the employee.

Support for Managing Retention

For *employee development* and *training* a job description:

▶ Contains the information we need to identify employees' development strengths and deficiencies.

▶ Tells what we need for individual development plans.

The Argument against Job Descriptions

Some organizations today believe that job descriptions are no longer useful. They want to base their staffing decisions on the skills of people, not the responsibilities of the job. Organizations like these are "person-based," and pay is based on skills. Employees are expected to take the initiative to pitch in, to do whatever needs to be done in order to achieve organizational success. Rather than have a specific set of tasks and job responsibilities, employees work on projects. When a project is over, the employee—often with the assistance of a mentor—finds another project. Anything that lists what employees are expected to do is thought to be confining and contrary to the culture. This is a climate of "the end of the job" and "only skills matter." These organizations counter the need for job descriptions with these arguments:

▶ Jobs disappear as work changes. Why maintain a job description if it will be outdated in a year or less?

▶ Evaluation plans give credit to the number of people supervised and the size of the budget. Why use an evaluation system that leads to hierarchy as we flatten our organization?

▶ Jobs are worth what the market says they are worth. Why determine pay from a job evaluation plan that is unrelated to the market?

▶ Employees can use job descriptions to say, "I don't have to do that assignment" or "It is not in my job description." Why should we limit ourselves?

Overall, job descriptions are a nuisance to prepare and have to be constantly revised. Why not skip this tedious process of keeping them up-to-date and assigning values and spend time on more productive activities?

The Argument for Job Descriptions

The naysayers have a point, but they are looking at job descriptions as if they existed for a narrow purpose and were written for the short term.

Job descriptions support the other processes that are part of the foundation of retention as well as our ability to manage retention. Figure 6.2 depicts those relationships. Here are responses to the specific items raised in "The Argument against Job Descriptions."

▶ A job description tells us why the job exists, the function that it serves for the organization. Tasks change frequently, but the reason for the job does not.

▶ We can develop job evaluation plans that do reflect our flatter, more nimble organizations. If we do want to use a traditional job evaluation plan, we can use job descriptions with other methods (such as broadbanding or market-pricing) that are aligned with our culture.

▶ We will always look at the market for pay, but may also want a method of pay that supports internal movement.

▶ As for employees who limit their contribution to the face value of their job description, they do not have the attitudes we want from our employees, and this problem has nothing to do with job descriptions.

In addition:

▶ We cannot lose sight of the value of telling employees their basic functions and general responsibilities.

▶ We must hold employees accountable for results.

▶ We need to emphasize skills to produce results, but we do not want to end up with a high-skills/low-results organization.

► Gives management information to plan career growth for high-potential employees.

► Gives employees information on content and requirements of other jobs.

For *compensation* a job description:

► Gives information to market-price the job.

► Holds data needed in an evaluation system.

For *performance management* a job description:

► Tells new employees their basic responsibilities and performance standards.

► Shows new employees how their job fits into the department's and organization's missions.

Figure 6.2   Job descriptions as a foundation for retention.

To meet *legal requirements* a job description:

▶ Gives information to determine if the job is exempt or nonexempt under the Fair Labor Standards Act (FLSA).

▶ Lists the essential and nonessential job functions for compliance with the Americans with Disabilities Act (ADA).

Building the Foundation

Like most foundations we build, this one does take work. We have to:

▶ Determine what constitutes the job.

▶ Collect and verify data.

▶ Identify the skills that really make a difference in performance.

The payoff for our work is substantial. Once we have a job description we are prepared for many of the other actions we take to retain employees. We will come back to job descriptions in other chapters of this book.

What Do Employees Think of Job Descriptions?

"It tells me what is expected of me."

"I see the breadth of my responsibilities."

"I can see where my work fits in with others'."

"If I think about posting on another job, the job description gives me an idea of what that work is like."

"I wasn't surprised that there was a lot of travel in my job since that was listed in the job description."

"It's useful to know the skills needed. I know I have good communication skills, which are really important on this job."

✍ Job Description

Basic Functions

General Duties and Responsibilities

Job Requirements
Skills

Education

Work Experience

Working Conditions

Skills and Behaviors

7

Retention Starts with Recruitment

We started building the foundation of retention with job descriptions. They tell us what the successful employee will do and the skills he or she will need in order to do it. Now we have to find that person.

In the past, this was not difficult to do. We put an ad in the newspaper or a sign in the window and found the employees we needed. Sure, there were some hard-to-fill positions. For them, we had to advertise more widely, go to job fairs, or use outside recruiters. For most positions, though, we had plenty of qualified applicants to choose from. Now, with our emphasis on employee skills, "hard-to-fill" applies to most positions.

One thing has not changed: Even then, potential employees evaluated the way they were treated. But in the past if we did not treat employees well and received a low score from them it did not matter. We still found enough people to work for us. Now it matters. Now, when we get a low score we cannot attract employees and we end up with unfilled positions. If we cannot fill the positions we do not have employees to retain. Now, recruitment is the first step to retention.

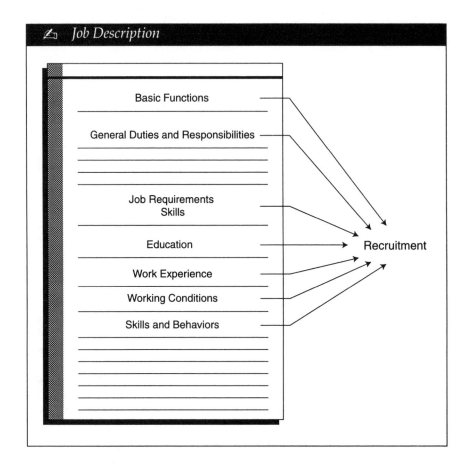

Recruitment Attracts the People We Want

Recruitment covers everything we do to create a candidate base for our open positions. In recruitment we:

▶ Search for potential employees.

▶ Find methods of communicating with them.

▶ Tell them about the position and our organization.

▶ Determine whether they have the skills we need.

▶ Describe how we can meet their career interests.

What Kinds of Things Do Potential Employees Say about Our Organization?

"I hear their Universal division is under a lot of pressure and starting to monitor everything people do."

"I asked their recruiter about the systems they use and he really seemed to know what he was talking about."

"They always seem to be involved with projects for kids. I like that."

"Their ads say competitive pay. That's true when you start but there aren't any incentives."

"They mention good benefits, but Marty went to work there and she says the benefits stink."

"I hear that their new projects aren't doing well and everyone is leaving."

"They don't care when you work as long as you get your work done."

"I saw they just were fined for polluting the river—not my kind of company."

We "meet" large numbers of people when we recruit—in print; by telephone, mail, e-mail, fax; or in person. It is important to treat each of them as a customer. The better prepared we are the better our results. Here are lists of the information, material, and resources that are useful to have handy.

GETTING STARTED

▶ Personnel requisition form for organizational and other data that links to all aspects of the position.

▶ Job descriptions.

▶ Affirmative action plan.

FINDING POTENTIAL EMPLOYEES

▶ Advertising agencies.

▶ External or executive recruiters.

▶ Media—a prepared list with data on effectiveness, audience, cost, contact names and numbers, and deadlines.

▶ Standard format of ads.

▶ Relationships with educational institutions, which provide mutual support: We supply services such as placements or support of their career programs while we get both the opportunity to become known as an employer and access to students.

▶ Relationships with placement organizations such as outplacement services and career centers.

▶ Relationships with union leadership who have sources of potential employees.

SOMETHING TO HAND OUT

▶ Recruiting package—a preassembled packet of material to tell potential employees:

Who we are.
What we do.
Why it is great to work here.

▶ Compensation policy.

▶ Work and family programs.

▶ Relocation policy.

▶ Benefits options and the extent of organizational contribution.

▶ Technology resources available to employees.

BACKUP

▶ Referral programs.

▶ Market data on pay.

▶ Guidelines on hiring bonuses.

▶ Contact lists with telephone, e-mail, and fax numbers for everyone we deal with.

▶ Published material on the organization and its practices (see Chapter 9, "Retention Starts with Orientation").

> ### We Would Never Treat Our Business Customers This Way!
>
> ▶ Potential employees send resumes in response to an ad and never hear from us.
> ▶ They talk to recruiters at job fairs who seem interested but never call.
> ▶ They have an informal chat with a manager who says, "You are just what we are looking for," and never follows up.
> ▶ They are asked to call back in a week and then told to call back in another week. . . .
>
> The people we are talking with now may not be right for the current opening, but we may be interested in them for a different position later. In the future, when we become interested in them, they may have already decided that we are not the kind of place where they want to work.

Everything we do creates impressions that affect the opinions of the people we hope to hire and eventually retain. When we advertise, talk with potential employees, and give presentations at professional meetings, we are being evaluated. The way we speak of our organization, describe our open positions, and respond to telephone calls and resumes influences potential employees.

Our Customers and Their Questions

What are the people we recruit doing while we are looking for them? They may or may not be actively searching for a job. Probably they are not. But they are considering their career interests and the type of work environment that suits them. We can attract employees with our jobs and our work environment.

Potential employees ask a lot of questions. And we have to be prepared to answer them. See Figure 7.1 for questions employees might ask about working in an organization.

Figure 7.1   Ten questions employees may ask about working in our organization before they say "yes".

1. *Self-description.* What does the organization say about itself to customers, shareholders, employees, board, contributors/funders, residents, and so forth? Are the messages in publications such as annual reports and employee newsletters clear and consistent?

2. *Staffing.* How clear are job requirements? Does the organization recruit from a variety of sources to attract a diverse group of prospective employees? How searching are the interview questions? Are tests (written, job simulations, personality tests, etc.) part of the screening process? Are employees (the potential peers) involved?

3. *Mission/strategy.* Is there a clear statement of the purpose of the organization? How long has it been in place? How was the mission statement developed? How is it communicated? Is there a strategy with goals and timetables that supports the mission? Is there a process to monitor it? How often is it reviewed and revised in response to actual operations and environmental changes?

4. *Flexibility.* Are there flexible work arrangements that recognize the personal and professional needs of employees? Are there opportunities for flextime? Alternative work schedules? Telecommuting? Working at home? Are employees given time for professional education and other development? Are there opportunities to have fun at work?

5. *Employee development.* What is the philosophy of employee development? What opportunities are actually available? Is there a commitment to a minimum number of hours of training? Does the organization pay attention to soft skills such as problem solving as well as technical skills? Are there mentoring or other support systems?

6. *Job expectations.* How do employees learn what is expected of them? Do employees participate in setting expectations? Who has responsibility for monitoring progress? How do employees get feedback on how well they are doing? Does feedback come from customers? From peers? Do employees assess their own performance?

Figure 7.1   *(Continued)*

> 7. *Rewards.* Is there an established compensation philosophy? What is it and how is it communicated? How are salaries determined? Are there noncash rewards? Are there incentives for individual performance? Are there team or organization incentives?
>
> 8. *Supervision.* What is the role of supervisors? Are they bosses? Leaders? Coaches? Do they primarily do the same work as their staff or do they spend most of their time and effort on supervision? Do employees provide input on the performance of their supervisors?
>
> 9. *Teamwork.* Do employees work in teams? How is this reflected in setting and managing expectations? If teamwork is important, what efforts are made to train employees in team development? How are new employees integrated into existing teams?
>
> 10. *Respect.* Are employees provided with the information they need to do their job? Are employees asked for their ideas about improving work processes? About serving customers? Are diverse opinions encouraged? Are employees treated according to their contribution and abilities rather than their gender, ethnicity, and/or status (exempt/nonexempt)?

Our Answers

It is absolutely critical that we give prospective employees an accurate picture of our organization and jobs. Yes, we may lose stars who are looking for a work environment that is different from ours. But it is better to be accurate than to mislead. In the twenty-first century work environment, the worst mistake is to misrepresent what we offer. The skilled employee will seek a better fit between what he or she wants and what the organization really provides. We will be left with an open position and have to recruit all over again.

What Do New Employees Say When the Promise and the Actuality Are Not Aligned?

"Their pictures showed great-looking facilities but most of the offices are crummy."

"They say they offer good benefits. They are good if you are single, but healthcare coverage for my family is really expensive."

"The recruiter told me about an incentive compensation plan but I learned it is available in only a few departments, and not mine."

"They say it is a fast-paced environment but it turns out to be 'hurry up and wait.' "

"They do have a good training department, but my boss says there is too much work to do and won't let me sign up."

"They are small and talked about their 'family atmosphere.' That is because there are so many family members employed. If you are not a relative you are somewhat of an outsider."

8

Retention Starts with Selection

"Did you hear about the guy who applied for a proofreader's position and misspelled his name in the resume?" That old joke circulates among recruiters, employment representatives, and career counselors. They tell it to job seekers to impress them with the importance of everything they do when they apply for a job. Spelling counts; following instructions about a format for a resume counts; showing up on time for an interview counts. Especially when it is an employer's market, that is, when we have the power, we can afford to be very particular about the way potential employees present themselves. That has not changed. What has changed, though, is that in the twenty-first century employment relationship, prospective employees are looking at us the same way. And because they have as much to say as we do in the hiring decision, we have to pay close attention.

Potential Employees Do Discuss Their Experiences. Do You Recognize Your Organization in Any of the Following?

"They wouldn't give me a tour of the work area—said it was too messy."

"When I asked to see the location with the opening the supervisor took me over and showed me around."

"They flew me in the night before and when I arrived to meet the manager the next morning, I was told that the job had been filled."

"At first they appeared well organized. They gave me a timetable of the interview schedule. But then they changed three out of the four meetings without an explanation."

"There was a team interview. They took turns asking questions and taking notes. They seemed to work together really well."

"When we were in the elevator this man got on that everyone seemed to know. They introduced me to him, saying I was here for an interview. He said that he hoped I was getting my questions answered, gave me his card, and said to call or e-mail if I wanted to ask him something. I found out later that he was the president."

"I met with the manager and director together. Then the director pulled me aside and told me that she was very impressed with me, said that top management had decided to fire the manager, and asked if I would be interested in that job."

Finding the Match

Selection includes all of the actions we take to identify the person who best matches the requirements of our position and to negotiate a mutually satisfactory agreement.

We started building our foundation with our job description where we defined the responsibilities of the position and the skills needed. In Chapter 7, "Retention Starts with Recruitment," we gathered a group of potential employees who may have the skills we want. Now we narrow that number and select the person we want to hire and who wishes to work for us. We look at what we do from his or her perspective as well as our own.

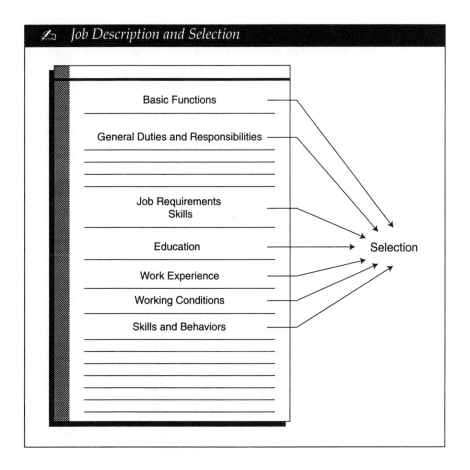

As in recruitment, we want to be prepared to treat potential employees as customers as they participate in selection. Here are lists of information and decisions that support an interview process. Having them ready before you contact a potential employee will enable you to treat him or her as a customer.

ADMINISTRATION

▶ Position file—maintains all the information and documentation on what we did to fill the job including the job description, tests, names of potential employees and reasons for their not being offered the position, and dates.

▶ Tracking system—monitors progress on all positions and provides references so we can see what we did the last time we filled the position.

▶ Timetable—sets overall schedule for stages in filling the position.

▶ Human resources management system—supports all steps and integrates data with other employee data systems.

STRATEGY

▶ Job priorities—prioritizes the skill requirements so we can focus on the essentials.

▶ Selection strategy—determines how to measure desired skills.

PARTICIPANTS

▶ Human resources or departmental representative—the point person who coordinates all stages of the selection process and communications with potential employees.

▶ Interviewers—those who share in gathering data (e.g., peers, direct reports, customers, human resources).

▶ External service providers—those who provide other services (e.g., assessors, physical abilities testing facility).

TESTS AND TESTING MATERIAL

▶ Resume screen—identifies people who may have the skills we are looking for.

▶ Tests—inventory of tests we have developed or purchased.

▶ Testing administration—decides the order in which tests are administered, including how decisions are made to move potential employees on to the next stage.

▶ Question data bank—enables us to tailor interviews to the position.

▶ Interview questionnaire—formats the questions including room for notes and scoring.

▶ Scoring system—provides consistency in assigning weights to responses.

▶ Reference checking—verifies information supplied by potential employees (e.g., education, prior work experience, driving record).

Selection Is a Two-Sided Relationship

An organization's selection process is characterized in the language used to describe it. After all, language reflects our attitude and the attitude is carried over to the way we act. Some of the phrases used are:

"We put candidates through hoops."

"Our tests are hurdles."

"We weed people out."

Potential Employees Have Their Own Checklists.
Here Is a Sample.

____ Information on the organization is up-to-date.
____ Schedule for site visit is provided before the first meeting.
____ Job expectations are clear.
____ I am told promptly of any delays or other problems in the schedule.
____ My time is respected.
____ They tell me the decision making timetable.
____ The training program is described in detail.
____ Information is provided on how pay is determined.
____ I have a chance to meet prospective coworkers and ask anything I want.
____ The people who interview me know how to conduct an interview.
____ My questions are answered to my satisfaction.
____ The organization has a strategy and appears to be following it.
____ The people I meet listen to what I say.

All of these imply a one-sided relationship. We are not the only ones with a relevant view, however. Potential employees are evaluating us. They are comparing us to their current employers and to others who are recruiting them. Think of selection in the new employment relationship as a merger: Both parties have something the other wants and seek to negotiate a mutually satisfactory agreement.

Selection Strategy

As we prepare for selection we have to determine the skills which are most important to successful job performance. The job description identifies the technical, management, and physical skills desired. Which are most critical? What is the best way to learn about potential employees' skills in those areas? We also want someone who has the right attitude and is reliable and honest. How do we evaluate that? In addition, we want the perfect person, someone who "can hit the ground running" and "walks on water." And, by the way, we need this person tomorrow. That is a lot to ask. Since we cannot get everything we have to decide what is important and what we will accept.

Whatever we decide will affect retention. How does testing affect retention? We can see how it works in the two most widely used tests: screening resumes and interviewing.

Resumes

This is the start of selection. All we know about potential employees to begin with is what they tell us. Our first step is to check and see if they claim to have what we want.

The traditional way to screen resumes was to compare the work experience and education with our requirements. The assumption was that if you had the work experience and education you could do the job. That was okay when it was easy to hire, and retention was not a problem. Now, in the twenty-first century employment environment, using work experience and education without looking at skills is too narrow an approach. It eliminates potential em-

A Variety of Education and Experience Prepares People for Our Positions

We are looking for an administrative assistant. The most important skill requirements are:

► Administrative skills—setting priorities for own work.
► Analysis—understanding underlying assumptions, not jumping to conclusions.
► Attention to detail—following up after handling problems and providing services.
► Communication—providing clear direction to others.
► Computer skills—maintaining data.

Qualified potential employees may include:

► Early retirees looking for a new career.
► Parents returning to the workforce once their children are in school.
► Graduates of two-year colleges looking for entry into a career that does not require technical knowledge.
► Graduates of retraining programs.

They may have the skills we want and might make high-performing employees even though their resumes do not contain the "right" words.

ployees who can bring breadth of knowledge as well as the skills we are looking for. For example:

► Experience in other industries or other sectors can bring exactly the skills we want and yet a fresh point of view.
► Experience in larger or smaller organizations can give us new ideas on how to handle our work.
► Knowledge gained outside of educational institutions brings a practical perspective to how work is performed.

We also risk eliminating people with the right skills and the potential for long-term employment with us when we use computer programs to screen resumes. The screening process itself is the problem. These programs look for the keywords entered by the recruiter and eliminate resumes without those words. This process works well when the search is for a particular license or certification (R.N., C.P.A.) or skill (one year of experience with Java, Spanish-speaking). It does not work if we are looking for an administrative assistant since (1) that title is used so differently in different organizations, and (2) the skills desired (analysis, communication) seldom appear in just those words on a resume. Having the right format and words for a resume becomes a position requirement.

Before we had computers, recruiters and human resources staff were accused of screening out resumes that did not contain the right words. Most of us, though, did take the time to read through resumes, especially when a position was hard to fill. Now, when it is hard to fill most positions, we rely more and more on a tool that does look for the right words. When we are having difficulty finding employees, we need to be more creative in our selection process.

Interviews

When we interview for skills, not work experience or job history, we avoid being distracted by where the interviewee gained experience. Our questions focus on what the interviewee has done in the past, how he or she demonstrated skills in situations similar to the ones characteristic of the new position. Questions often begin with, "Give me an example of a time when. . . ." We follow up with probes to get a complete picture of that past experience:

▶ What the person did.
▶ The circumstances surrounding the action.
▶ What happened as a result.

This method is described as behavioral, situational, or experiential interviewing. The interview questions are based on the skills in the job description; the behaviors in the job description virtually write interview questions. For example, analysis is one of the skills in the sample job description in Chapter 6, "Retention Starts with Job Descriptions." One behavior listed under "Analysis" is: "Understands assumptions underlying issues, and questions them." We can ask, "Give me an example of a time when you questioned assumptions made by others." Probes help us find out where it happened, what prompted the interviewee to question assumptions, what actions were taken, and what the results were. We want to learn about the skills and not just where and how they were gained.

Changing industries and careers is part of the twenty-first-century work environment. Employees tend not to narrow their choices about the type of organizations they wish to work in. They look for the place that fits with their career interests. We want employees who have the skills to do the work we need to have done. Artificial barriers can cause us to overlook people who can do that for us.

Other Tests

There are other tests we can use. Choosing the right ones requires a study of their validity for our purpose. We also have to remember that selection tests are predictors. There is no certainty to selection tests, only probabilities. Judiciously chosen, combinations of selection tests can increase our odds of selecting the right person. Figure 8.1 is a short list of other tests.

▶ *To Go Further*

Deems, *Hiring.*
Douglas, Feld, and Asquith, *Employment Testing Manual.*
Janz, Hellervik, and Gilmore, *Behavior Descriptive Interviewing.*
Smart, *The Smart Interviewer.*
Spencer and Spencer, *Competence at Work.*
Thornton, *Assessment Centers in Human Resource Management.*

See the Bibliography for citations.

Figure 8.1   Tests often used in selection, in addition to resumes and interviews.

Job Simulations   Testing ability to perform some aspect of the job. For example:

▶ Training analyst—gathers information on a request for training, identifies the needs, and makes a recommendation on how to meet them.

▶ Graphic artist—takes the pictures and articles provided and designs a newsletter.

▶ Community relations specialist—reviews material on an issue that may disturb the community and develops a strategy that effectively advocates the organization's position.

Assessment Exercises   Samples of behaviors in typical situations:

▶ Supervisor—dealing with a difficult employee.

▶ Customer service positions—dealing with a difficult customer.

▶ Any position—taking material provided and preparing a 10-minute oral presentation using a flip chart.

▶ Any position—handling an in basket.

Performance Tests   Testing technical knowledge and ability valid for job performance:

▶ Personal computer (PC) skills—performance test of typical job duties.

▶ Writing—preparation of a two-page paper summarizing materials provided.

▶ Blueprint reading—following blueprints to construct an object.

▶ Accounting—take data and prepare an income statement.

Basic Skills Tests   Including some with audio or audiovisual prompts:

▶ Listening skills.

▶ Verbal ability.

▶ Mental ability.

Figure 8.1 *(Continued)*

> ▶ Spatial relationships ability.
>
> ▶ Mathematical reasoning.
>
> ▶ Supervisory actions, responding to questions based on scenarios viewed.
>
> **Personality and Traits Tests**
>
> ▶ Honesty.
>
> ▶ Reliability.
>
> ▶ Assertiveness.
>
> ▶ Initiative.
>
> ▶ Group orientation.
>
> **Assessment Centers**   Evaluating demonstrated behavior in a wide range of skills. Their use is often confined to leadership positions because they are expensive. They have been used in staffing for blue-collar and white-collar jobs in new facilities that are looking for employees who can work in teams.

Negotiating the Offer

The way we negotiate reflects our organization and gives the potential employee a picture of how we do things. Selection is a form of merger with each side having something to gain and something to lose. We all have seen mergers between two organizations that did not work. The cultures may be too different, the systems may not communicate with each other, or the styles of the remaining executives may clash, with the result that the merger was not productive. The difficulties were often apparent in the negotiations. The same events can happen when we negotiate an offer. Since retention starts with selection, we want the negotiations to result in a positive picture of our organization.

Once we have successfully completed negotiations, we have a new employee and are ready to start retaining the employee with orientation.

9

Retention Starts with Orientation

The courtship is over. We chose Richard because our selection process predicted that he was the best match with our position requirements. We and Richard have agreed to the conditions of employment, including the work, pay, benefits, and starting date. From our perspective we have successfully recruited a new employee. We have a short period of time before Richard assumes his new responsibilities with us. During that time Richard will develop an impression of us and what his new job will be like. We need to influence that impression and begin to integrate him into our organization. Now that Richard is planning to join us, retention starts with new employee orientation.

New employee orientation begins the moment the agreement is reached and continues through the first several days of employment. During this time we:

▶ Show appreciation that Richard will be joining us.

▶ Answer questions.

▶ Deal with physical examinations, relocation, requests for documents, and whatever else we need to take care of before the first day at work.

▶ Enroll Richard in benefits.

▶ Tell him the practical things he needs to know.

▶ Provide him with the resources he needs to do his work.

Maintaining Relationships with Our New Employee

Even the most confident people have some difficulty in making changes. They are leaving the known for the unknown. Even if the known was not very good, they still knew how to navigate within it. As the employer we want to maintain our connections with Richard so we can respond if there are doubts. Doubts can be created by the way we treat our new employee in this interim period between the time we agreed on his employment with us and his first day of work.

"Even before I signed the offer letter, I received a call from the president inviting me to join the organization."

"Once we agreed on the terms I began to get telephone calls and e-mail from the supervisor and members of the work group welcoming me."

"I was scheduled to start on January 3. They invited me to the holiday party in December so I could meet everyone."

"I got a big package from them right after I accepted the offer. There was a T-shirt, a cap, and a new planner with their logo."

"I was really pleased that whenever I called with a question on benefits I got a prompt reply."

"I started in mid-January. The healthcare benefit was different than I had been told—apparently there were changes at the beginning of the year and someone 'forgot' to tell me."

Throughout, Richard is our customer. We want Richard to be sure that he has made a good decision in agreeing to work for us. We want to anticipate his questions on a broad range of topics. We want to tell him more about our organization and its business operations, policies, and benefits. We have a lot to do.

If we are a nonprofit and Richard a volunteer, we do many of the same things. Volunteers have the same need for practical information as paid staff. They need job descriptions and forms to report their hours. Most importantly they need information on how their work connects to the mission of the organization. Their enthusiasm and empathy for the good that the organization does are what attracted them. That spirit can wear off. Treating volunteers as customers creates ties that maintain their interest and involvement.

Our Employee, Our Customer

New employee orientation is one of the foundations of retention. We need to be prepared for employees at different locations, in different levels of the organization, and most importantly, with different individual needs. We need careful planning and preparation to identify all the individualized paperwork they need to sign and the specific information required for their circumstances. In getting ready for orientation we can follow the methods that our marketing department uses to reach and retain customers for our products and services:

▶ Consider the customer's (new employee's) perspective.

▶ Specify objectives.

▶ Develop key messages and delivery methods.

▶ Prepare to respond to the unexpected.

▶ Keep information current.

▶ Assign responsibility.

Here is a planning list for orientation:

PREPARATION

▶ Road map and timetable of what the employee can expect between the date of agreement to the offer and the end of orientation.

▶ Checklist of the decisions on benefits the new employee will have to make the first few days and the material that explains his or her options.

▶ Checklist of the information the new hire must bring the first day, and why.

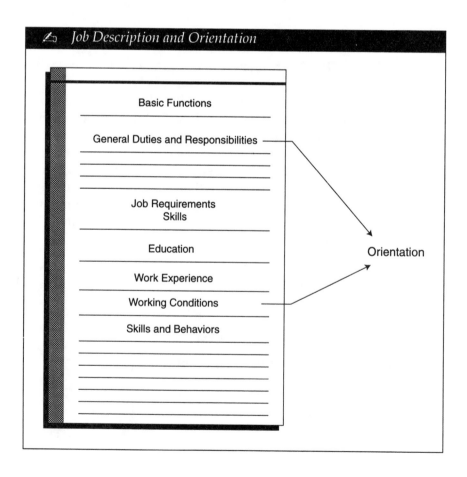

OVERVIEW

▶ Personal welcome from chief executive officer (CEO).

▶ Mission statement.

▶ Annual report.

▶ Employee handbook.

▶ Collective bargaining agreements.

▶ Big brother/big sister program.

▶ Tour of facilities.

FORMS

▶ Personal information.

▶ Personalized forms for benefits enrollments.

▶ I-9, W-4, direct deposit, and other forms.

GETTING STARTED

▶ Map of organization's locations and directions to them.

▶ Samples of products.

▶ Employee publications.

▶ Information on funders.

▶ Schedule of group orientation sessions.

▶ Organization chart.

▶ Pictures of key leaders.

▶ Computer and other passwords.

▶ Telephone book, including locations, and e-mail addresses.

▶ Attendance expectations.

▶ Planner with pages on the organization.

ABOUT THE JOB

▶ Job description.

▶ Career opportunity services.

▶ Mentoring program.

▶ Individual development services.

▶ Feedback tools used to assist in development.

▶ Appreciation programs.

▶ Compensation philosophy and details.

▶ Employee incentive compensation plan.

▶ Performance management process.

▶ Training catalog.

ORIENTING TO THE WORKPLACE

▶ Flextime policies.

▶ Neighborhood features.

▶ Fitness facilities, on-site or nearby.

▶ On-site services.

▶ Opportunities for involvement with volunteer and community programs.

▶ Recreation facilities.

▶ Restaurants in the neighborhood.

▶ Gift certificates for nearby restaurants.

▶ Gift certificate for the new employee to go to lunch with new peers.

FUN

▶ Video to take home to show the family.

▶ Work and family programs.

▶ T-shirt with logo.

▶ Sports leagues/teams sign-up sheets.

▶ Invitation to annual picnic/event.

EVALUATION OF ORIENTATION

▶ Evaluation process.

▶ Evaluation forms.

Preparing for the First Day of Work

The most difficult part of orientation, for both Richard and us, is the first day at work. There are a lot of formalities. We need to complete I-9s and tax forms, have him sign up for benefits, review our equal employment opportunity (EEO) and sexual harassment policies, and ask him to sign for receipt of our employee handbook.

At the same time, his supervisor is waiting for him to start. It has taken a long time to fill the position and there is a lot of work waiting for Richard. Richard also wants to get started on his new job and he has his own agenda of what he wants to learn.

What We Want to Hear Employees Say about Orientation

"They sent me a lot of information on benefits before I started. It gave me a chance to discuss them with my husband and it was easier to make decisions."

"In orientation they brought in a group of employees who had been there about three months. They were able to tell us about some of the things that they learned that weren't in the books. That was really helpful."

"Before I started I got a package with all the forms that had to be completed. An HR rep called a day or two later and answered all of my questions."

"They sent me a video about the organization. I think the idea was to share it with my family. My three-year-old was really excited. 'That's mommy's new office!' he said."

"They have a series of lunchtime programs once a week about different aspects of the business. They gave me the schedule during orientation and encouraged me to attend. My new supervisor backed that up. She said she would be sure I was free to go."

Telling about Our Organization

Companies that hire many people at one time can involve them in a multiday group session with speakers and facilitators who introduce new employees to the values and beliefs of the organization. But many of us hire new employees in small groups or one at a time, making it much harder to bring in officers or other speakers to cover information in depth. A smaller organization might use methods like these to help employees learn:

▶ Monthly or bimonthly two-hour sessions with organization leaders on key topics, open to everyone hired in the past 12 months.

▶ Full day sessions, scheduled twice a year, for everyone hired in the past six months.

▶ Programmed learning that asks new employees to seek answers to key questions from organization leaders.

▶ Orientation mentor who works one-on-one with the new employee.

▶ Department open houses with demonstrations of what they do, for new and current employees.

▶ Games, like treasure hunts, that ask employees to visit certain areas and bring back items that represent those operations.

We also want to tell employees about our informal practices. They are the things that everyone who has been around for a while knows and takes for granted. Current employees do not think of them as issues, but they can bother new employees. Answers to the following can be put together in a FAQ (Frequently Asked Questions) format.

"How much choice do you have in scheduling vacations?"

"Where else can I park? How much do I have to pay?"

"How flexible is the department about lunch?"

"How is performance really measured?"

"Does the staff go out for lunch as a group?"

"Is there a place nearby where I can work out?"

"When do I get paid? Is there a lag in pay or am I paid to date?"

"What has been the payout in your incentive plan in the past three years?"

"What are the expectations about coming to work in really bad weather?"

"What attitude will people have if I leave work in the middle of the day to pick up my child when he is sick?"

"How willing are employees to share information with people in other departments?"

"Do people care when I work as long as I get my work done?"

Evaluating Orientation

Evaluating orientation gives us the chance to see how well we are doing and what we can change. A two-part evaluation is particularly useful. A first evaluation immediately after the formal orientation tells us what we can consider changing right away. A second, after three months, tells how well the orientation works to integrate employees into the organization.

The payoff from being prepared comes when we realize that we have what we need to welcome new employees into the organization and do not have to figure out what we need to do each time. A bigger payoff comes when we cut down the amount of time it takes for new employees to understand the organization and how to work within it. They can start contributing earlier and be productive earlier. If we continue to treat them well and they get what they are looking for from us, they will stay longer.

III

Managing Retention

10

Managing Retention

W e were asked about retention as we were interviewing a potential employee. We had not even made an offer, let alone hired her, and Doris asked us, "What will you do to retain me?"

What do we as employers say in response? We know what *not* to say. She is not interested in a recitation of what we put in our recruiting material. She is not looking for a "program." She wants to know what she, Doris, will get in return for the skills, knowledge, and creativity she contributes.

Part III has answers to managing retention.

The first response that comes to mind is money. Money is a part of organizational life, sometimes even when we are not talking about it. Money includes salary, incentives, noncash awards, and benefits, and each of those categories provides ways to respond to Doris's question.

Then we look at career opportunities. Money and career are the two top concerns for employees as they consider staying or leaving. The area of career opportunities includes the availability of feedback and development planning, nontraditional training, and the opportunities for changing jobs within the organization. Again, each gives us something to say to Doris.

The next area is our work environment. It includes our policies and procedures and the supervisors and management who interpret them. Our policies are our statements of how we treat people. Doris wants to know what we say. She also wants to know what we do—how supervisors really treat employees, and how employees treat each other.

From there we look at performance management. Although sometimes it is grouped with development and at other times with money, here performance management provides its own answer to Doris.

The next area is work and family. Flexibility in when and where work is performed is important in employee decision making about staying or leaving. Doris wants to know what our current practices are as well as what our culture supports.

The last chapter in this section on managing retention is on

Figure 10.1   Retention at the center of the organization and its business strategy.

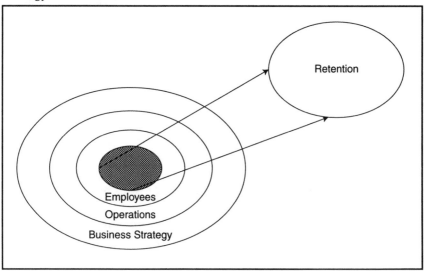

counteroffers and their place in the twenty-first century employment relationship.

Figure 10.1 shows retention at the core of business strategy. If we cannot retain the employees we want to keep, then our operations will not operate and our strategies will fail. Here are tools to help you keep the employees you want to retain.

11

Let's Talk about Money

$\mathbf{M}$oney is a universal topic around the workplace. We have to talk about it here, too. Before we relate money to retention in particular we have to understand how it fits into everyday organizational life.

How many different pay practices do you have in your organization? It was not too long ago that the only form of money that most employees received was what we now call *base pay*. Base pay refers to the salary and wages that the employer agrees to pay. Pay grew with general increases or step progressions, promotions, or reclassifications. Occasionally, organizations used profit sharing, gainsharing, and other experiments. The only extra may have been $10 or a turkey or ham at Christmas. Pay was simple, straightforward, and easy to administer.

Now we have a variety of pay practices, each intended to achieve a different result. We want to reward employees for working in teams, and, at the same time, for being resourceful individual contributors. We pay employees for learning new skills and also for achieving project targets. We have annual incentive plans that pay for meeting organizational goals and, at the same time, spot awards for special efforts. Here is a list of some of the reasons for receiving pay:

BASE PAY

▶ Salary and wages—pay for being at work.

INCREASES FOR DEMONSTRATING SKILLS

▶ Competency pay—demonstrating and using a new competency.

▶ Skill-based pay—demonstrating and using a new skill.

▶ Job progression—moving up in responsibility within a technical or professional area.

INCREASES FOR RESULTS

▶ Incentive—for results achieved against a target.

▶ Commission—a percentage of sales.

▶ Gainsharing—cost saving, additional production, or similar results.

▶ Merit increase—individual quantitative and qualitative results achieved.

PAY FOR WORKING MORE HOURS OR BEING PREPARED TO WORK MORE HOURS

▶ Overtime—for hours worked over 40 per week, or other basis used by the organization.

▶ On-call pay—for being available for work even if not called in to work.

▶ Premium pay—usually double or even triple the hourly rate, for working on holidays, weekends, or other similar special circumstances.

INCREASES NOT DEPENDENT ON PERFORMANCE OR NEW SKILLS OR ANYTHING ELSE

▶ Cost of living allowance (COLA)—to "keep employees whole."

▶ General increase—something for everyone.

INCREASES BASED ON THE ORGANIZATION'S FINANCIAL SUCCESS

▶ Profit sharing—payout from our profits.

▶ Bonus—an "extra" when we have the cash.

OTHER FORMS OF INCREASES

▶ Promotional increase—for assuming new and higher-level responsibilities.

▶ Market adjustment—in response to competitive pressures in the labor market.

▶ Suggestion system—for ideas that make a difference.

▶ Spot award—doing something unexpected.

Pay used to be about the same amount in each pay period. It might vary because of overtime pay, but otherwise it stayed constant until the next general increase or promotion. Now we also have:

▶ Variable pay—money given as a lump sum payment. It cannot be counted on from year to year because it has to be earned anew each year. Another term for variable pay is "pay at risk."

▶ Stock options—money that may or may not be received at some future date. The value is unknown because it depends on the vesting period, exercise price, and future performance of the company's stock. There is more about stock options later in this chapter.

▶ Deferred compensation—money that is earned in one time period and, under the terms by which it is earned, not to be paid out until a future time period.

A Peek at an Employee's Annual Earnings

At the beginning of the year Jim sat down with his W-2 form and tried to figure out what the numbers meant. He wanted to reconcile what he saw on the form with the money he had received.

▶ His base pay at the beginning of last year was $30,000.
▶ He received a 6% increase in April and a 5% competency adjustment in July, so he should have three months at $30,000, three months at $31,800, and six months at $33,390, for a total of $32,145.
▶ That didn't match the W-2.
▶ Then he remembered some additional income:
  The $500 incentive he received in October on the start-up of the new facility.
  The $900 from the annual incentive plan.
  The $50 certificate for dinner for two, received for his suggestion on helping customers by adding more signs.
  The $245 for on-call pay during the last few weeks of the project.
▶ Still not right.
▶ There were the pretax deductions. Now Jim subtracted:
  The 7% of base contribution to his 401(k).
  The $185 per month payment for the health maintenance organization (HMO).
▶ That was better, but he was still off by $50. Then he remembered that the $50 spot award was under some dollar limit and wasn't taxed.

It Is Money Even When We Do Not Use the Word

There are times when we want to avoid talking about money. We want to do something for an employee that does not include pay. Still, money is in the background of the discussion. For example:

▶ We talk about motivating an employee by offering a great opportunity to learn a new technology and develop new skills. We will describe that opportunity but make clear that there is no pay increase, for now. We are compensating the employee with development instead of money.

Benefits Equal Money

While talking about substitutes for money we cannot forget the biggest ones—benefits. Benefits include healthcare, vacations and other time off, life insurance, pension, matching contributions to a 401(k) or 403(b), plus unemployment compensation, workers compensation, and Social Security. All these and more provide compensation to employees at a cost that is not obvious to them but a major one to us.

▶ We understand that it is important to express appreciation for a job well done. We call that a noncash award. Our language implies that the usual award is money.

▶ We tell employees that one of the advantages of working here is that our vacation benefit is substantial. The unspoken corollary is that time off from work is given to make up for low pay.

So, even when we are not explicitly mentioning "money" we are in effect talking about money.

Besides nonmonetary rewards, we can give money to employees in different ways. Directly:

▶ We want to keep John through the end of a project. We offer him a $7500 retention incentive if he stays for the next 13 months. There is more on retention bonuses later on in the chapter.

▶ We have high turnover in our customer service representative jobs. After we train them, they leave for more money. We create a higher-level position that pays a dollar an hour more, and promote customer service reps to that new level when they successfully complete training, including performance tests.

▶ The manager thinks that Marie is restless in her job and is talking with recruiters. He speeds up her promotion to the level of senior engineer and gives her a project that he knows she wants.

Or indirectly:

▶ We send Joan to a professional conference that happens to be at a ski resort—she loves to ski.

▶ The soccer team Sam coaches won the local championship and is now going to the regionals. We give him time off with pay so he doesn't have to use his vacation days.

▶ Our employee survey said that "having the latest technology" is a predictor of job satisfaction. We buy new equipment for its productive capacity and to keep employees who want "the latest" happy.

▶ That same survey identified the interest of employees in having fitness facilities on-site. We converted unused space to a fitness facility so employees can work out on their lunch hour.

▶ Jane wants to do a project for her college course on quality measurement. We give her time off from her regular tasks to work on the project. At the end of the semester we ask her to work with us to implement it.

Making Sense of Pay

Where did all of these pay practices come from? We did not plan to have such a variety. We added them in response to union negotiations, competitive market conditions, management requests, or as part of a reward strategy to support organizational goals. Productivity incentives such as gainsharing or Scanlon plans go back to the 1930s. Cash incentives and stock options have been used in executive compensation for many years and are now becoming more prevalent at all levels of our organizations. Signing bonuses—giving money to someone to agree to come to work for us—is another practice that has spread. At one time it was used in a few specialized professional and sales jobs.

Now the practice is used for new college graduates and hard-to-fill technical and customer service jobs.

Every time we add a pay practice that makes economic sense for one group of employees, we are perceived to put other employees at a disadvantage. Employees who thought that their pay was okay become dissatisfied with it when they learn about opportunities for pay that they cannot share in. Having a variety of reasons for paying employees inevitably creates invidious comparisons. After a while we find ourselves with a number of pay practices that do not seem to work for us. They:

▶ Have conflicting goals.

▶ Are hard to administer.

▶ Increase labor costs more than we think they should.

▶ Are not consistent with our mission and values.

▶ Confuse employees.

▶ Cause morale problems between the haves and have-nots.

Do We Get What We Pay For?

Money is important, but the impact of many of our pay practices is unpredictable. We are never sure if we are paying for something we could have achieved even if we were not paying for it. We introduced each of these pay practices to achieve an objective. Did we reach it? It is hard to know. If we have a limited objective we may be able to measure our results. If we use retention bonuses, we can calculate the percentage of employees who stay for the retention period. Most of the time, though, our purposes are more general and vague. We institute pay practices to:

▶ Motivate employees to be productive, with merit programs or incentive plans.

▶ Send a message about what is important to the organization (e.g., improving customer service, improving our safety record).

These objectives are affected by many factors within our complex organizations. And, despite much research and study on pay, the academic and professional literature does not give us much guidance on the effectiveness of any particular method.

Money as Motivator

Does money motivate employees to perform? If we say we are willing to pay for a behavior or a result, will we get it? In the past several years there has been an animated discussion on money and motivation propelled by the work of Alfie Kohn. His provoca-

---

What Do Employees Say about Pay? How Does It Figure in Their Personal Calculations about Staying or Leaving?

"I want money. I am going to go wherever I get the most."

"The pay wasn't great but at least my boss treated me well and tried to get me the training I needed. My new boss has no clue to what we need here. I'm leaving."

"The signing bonus really influenced my decision to come here."

"They call it 'pay for performance' but it takes more than a three percent increase to motivate me."

"They bring in the new people at higher pay than I get. I like my job, but the pay difference bothers me."

"They want to base our pay on the team. I understand that we have to work together but Pam just doesn't get it. We spend a lot of time explaining things to her and working around her. Yet, she will get the same increase as the rest of us. It isn't fair."

"The pay is okay but the benefits, especially the 401(k), are really what keep me here."

"I know that the pay is low but I really believe in what we are doing. It gives me a lot of satisfaction to do some good in the world."

tively titled book, *Punished by Rewards: The Trouble with Gold Stars, Incentive Plan$, A's, Praise, and Other Bribes,* has led to extensive debate in business and professional journals. The questions about money and motivation are:

▶ Does money motivate at all?

▶ Does money demotivate?

▶ If money motivates, what behaviors or results does it influence?

▶ If money motivates, how long does the influence last?

What emerges from the research and discussion is that motivation is a complicated concept and that any plan based on simplistic assumptions will not work for very long. My own conclusion is that the research shows some support for rewards motivating *quantitative* performance in the *short term.* For example, we can use incentives to increase the number of customers an employee serves in a week, assuming (1) the employee has the skills to do so, and (2) money is valued. The focus on numbers of customers does not describe most of the work in our organizations. We also want our employees to provide good customer service week after week.

In most jobs today we want employees at all levels to undertake complex assignments whose results are known only in the long term.

▶ *To Go Further*

Gupta and Shaw, "Let the Evidence Speak."
Kohn, "Challenging Behaviorist Dogma."
Kohn, *Punished by Rewards.*

See the Bibliography for citations.

Money as Messenger

An alternative idea to "money as motivator" is "money as messenger." The way we distribute money tells employees what we value in our organizations. The phrase "follow the money" means that if we know how management distributes money we know what management really wants. Here are examples of messages we send:

- ▶ *Customer service.* An incentive plan that pays employees 2% of salary for improving customer service may not motivate, but it does tell everyone what the organization values.
- ▶ *Development.* An organization that gives employees $1000 to spend on development, subject to minimal supervisory approval, communicates that development is important.
- ▶ *Trust.* When we tell frontline employees that they can authorize expenditures up to $100 to help a customer, we show more trust than if they have a $25 limit or if all requests must be approved.
- ▶ *Pay for performance.* A 4% merit budget with awards ranging from 2% to 6% tells employees:

  We do not recognize wide differences in performance.
  If your performance is highly rated your reward is recognition and not money.
  If your performance is low-rated, then you will not get a big increase; but don't worry—you will get something.

- ▶ *Focus.* If employees can get a bigger financial reward soliciting funds for an organized charity than they can for good performance in our organization, then the message is that skill in raising funds for an outside organization is more important than skills needed for the job.

The messages tell employees how they will be paid. If the organization pays for good customer service, then employees can decide if they want to work in an organization that puts its money into customer service. If the organization keeps base pay stable and uses variable pay such as incentives to reward performance, then it puts pay at risk. Employees can decide if that meets their needs.

Bringing Coherence to Pay and Pay Strategy

It would be nice if we could erase all of our current practices and start over. That way we could decide how we wanted to use our money and design methods that carried out our objectives. However, we cannot really start over; our pay practices are too entangled in our culture. We can change our practices, but slowly. We can step back and think through how to use money to support our organization's business strategy. We can develop a philosophy of how we want to use our money. If we do that, the next time someone suggests a new pay method we can consider if, and how, it fits into what we already do.

Developing a Compensation Philosophy

We want to use money to:

▶ Support our business strategy.
▶ Be relevant to our employees.
▶ Connect to our working conditions.

A compensation philosophy is our statement of how we want to pay employees. It gives us a framework to guide decisions on selecting and implementing pay practices. Within the framework we can develop targeted responses to particular circumstances.

Here are two statements of compensation philosophy. The pay practices developed from them will be markedly different.

First, internally focused:

It is our policy to maintain a salary administration program (SAP) so that all employees are compensated fairly and equitably, consistent with the individual's assigned duties and responsibilities. We maintain internal equity by valuing our jobs according to a common evaluation plan that systematically recognizes differences in job value. We evaluate market data for our industry and set pay to attract and

retain employees. We reward each employee proportionately to the value of the employee's contribution and our ability to pay.
Our objectives are:

▶ Pay employees based on the value of their assigned responsibilities, per our evaluation plan.

▶ Reward outstanding performance.

▶ Pay salaries that enable us to attract, motivate, and retain qualified individuals who can contribute to our goals.

▶ Support employees who wish and are able to assume greater responsibilities by providing noncompetitive reclassification.

Second, market-driven:

Our ability to grow and prosper depends on being able to recruit, motivate, and retain the best people in our industry. The pay we offer is competitively high in the market for the talented professionals we want to attract. We motivate our employees by giving them challenging work and resources to do that work. We reward employees according to their contribution to our success. All employees have a stake in our future.

As we design our own philosophy we want it to line up with our business strategy. Variables we are concerned with exist on a continuum:

Equity

Internal———————————————————————External

Labor as a percentage of our cost of doing business

High———————————————————————Low

Pay at risk

High———————————————————————Low

Pay for performance (merit)

Yes ———————————————————————No

Pay based on

Responsibilities ———————————————————————Skills

> ▶ To Go Further

Chingos and Peat Marwick, *Paying for Performance.*
Fay and Risher, *New Strategies for Public Pay.*
Flannery, Hofrichter, and Platten, *People, Performance, & Pay.*
Lawler, *Strategic Pay.*
McAdams, *The Reward Plan Advantage.*
Nelson, *1001 Ways to Reward Employees.*
Pfeffer, *The Human Equation.*
Schuster and Zingheim, *The New Pay.*
Wilson, *Innovative Reward Systems for the Changing Workplace.*

See the Bibliography for citations.

Once we decide where we want to be on those lines, we can choose pay practices to implement our philosophy. The methods we choose answer the question, "What will you do to retain me?" The remainder of this chapter examines responses in four areas:

1. Salary.
2. Incentives.
3. Appreciation.
4. Benefits.

Salary

"What will you do to retain me?"
"I will pay you well."

Salary or wages is what most of us use for our everyday living expenses. We may count on having extras. Overtime pay may have been steady for the past year and is expected to continue. Incentives have paid off for the past three years and this year should be no different. Still, our regular salary or wages is the one part of our pay we can rely on.

Surveys show that salary ranks high on employees' lists of what keeps them with their employer. The "Survey of Factors Influencing Employees to Stay With or Leave Their Employers" (see Chapter 18) showed:

Attractors (factors that make employees want to stay):

"Salary"—5th place, 47%.

Preventers (factors that keep employees from leaving):

"Do not believe I can match my pay"—4th place, 20%.

"Unable to match my pay elsewhere"—10th place, 13%.

Reasons for leaving previous job:

"Was not paid what I was worth"—4th place, 22%.

"Could not live on the pay"—6th place, 20%.

Employees think salary is important. Employers agree. Surveys of pay practices report that employers consider compensation (and benefits) an important and often the most important part of their retention strategy. The Bibliography lists several recent surveys. The question asked of us is: Since salary is so important, how do we get it right? How do we determine salaries that retain employees?

Our compensation philosophy helps us determine the relative importance of salary in the total compensation our employees may receive. It tells employees what we pay for and how we do so. Employees come to work for us because there is a match between our philosophy and what they want. What do they look for, now that they have made the decision to work for us?

What Do Employees Want?

Although some of the employees we want to retain will chase money and are always looking for more, most employees want to be paid well for what they do, but not necessarily be the highest paid. They have a concept of fair pay based on:

1. The kind of organization, acknowledging differences caused by:

   Sector—for-profits, nonprofits, government.

   Industry—retail, manufacturing, banking, transportation, and so on.

   Trade-offs—between base pay and other rewards (for example, working conditions, benefits, time off).

2. Comparisons with:

   Other jobs in the same organization (internal equity).

   Comparable jobs in other organizations (external equity).

   One's own performance.

   What friends and colleagues with the same background and education earn.

Employees want our reasons for pay decisions to be consistent with what we say they will be. When they joined us they decided that our pay methods matched their needs. They have seen us

---

One Way to Cause Dissatisfaction

Many organizations describe their compensation philosophy like this:

- ▶ Minimum—the pay for employees entering the job.
- ▶ Midpoint—pay for experienced employees who can satisfactorily perform all aspects of the job.
- ▶ Maximum—the most that the organization will pay.

If we say this and then move salary ranges upward at the same time we give salary increases, employees make slow progress in moving higher in the salary range. It often takes a very long time for the pay of an experienced employee who can satisfactorily perform all aspects of the job to reach the midpoint. The employee's actual circumstances are out of step with the policy and the employee becomes disillusioned. The discrepancy is a cause of distrust and dissatisfaction.

make changes and continue to stay with us because the fit between what we offer and what they want is satisfactory. Within that framework, as long as the employee's salary is in the expected range and we follow our own policies, pay is okay and not a cause of dissatisfaction and departure from the organization.

What Do We Want?

Alternatives to consider in paying salary and wages include:

▶ *Pay according to the market.* Pay is competitive in our labor market. "Competitive" usually means the middle of the market, but we can define it for our purposes as the 75th percentile or the 40th. We can also determine the organizations, industries, and locations that comprise the labor market.

▶ *Pay for assigned responsibilities.* Pay is based on a job evaluation plan that represents the values of job factors to the organization. It may or may not include grades or bands. Pay for jobs that are today's hot skills is handled through variable pay, such as lump sums, that are kept outside the structure.

▶ *Pay for core competencies.* We identify the key competencies and associated behaviors for all employees and put a value on them. Technical skills can be used as a modifier, to reflect a market that pays more for engineers than technical assistants, even if the technical assistant has better communication and customer service skills than the engineer.

▶ *Pay the person, not the job.* We look at the employee's skills and their value to us. Skills may be in addition to the core competencies valued by the organization, or instead of them if we do not have core competencies.

We can use more than one method, if our culture allows. We can have multiple job evaluation plans. We can have different sets of competencies for different job families or levels in the organization. We can pay for technical competencies at the market and soft skills according to our internal values. And we can decide to pay

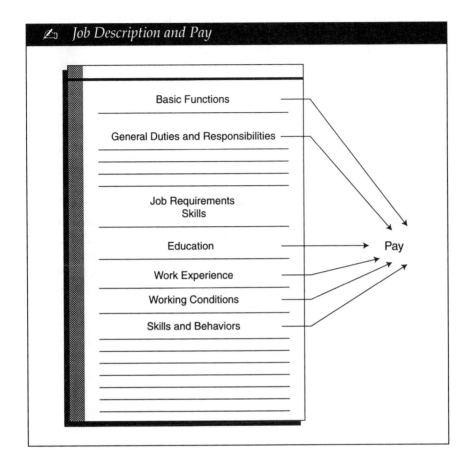

for exceptions to our philosophy as variable pay, giving lump sums instead of increasing base pay.

Our compensation philosophy guides decisions on pay practices. Internally focused organizations emphasize pay for assigned responsibilities. Increases will be based on changes in the cost of living. There will be a struggle between internal equity and the pay needed to recruit and retain employees with hot skills.

The organization that is market-driven in its business will be market-driven in its pay practices. It will pay people for their skills at the market. It may have grades, or bands, and salary administration policies. There will be a great deal of flexibility in how those policies are administered.

Communicating Pay

When we tell employees about our compensation policy and pay practices we create the basis for employee perceptions of those practices. Employees want to be treated fairly and equitably. Those words, "fairly" and "equitably," are abstract concepts. They need definition. We can supply the definitions for our organization as we tell employees what we pay for and why.

The method we use to pay employees is often a hidden topic. Some organizations do not publish pay ranges, or they give the information only to supervisors. Job evaluation plans are almost always kept confidential. But, there are very few secrets in organizations. Some employees always know the information, and others think, correctly or incorrectly, that they do know. The more we decide to tell employees about our pay practices, the better we will be able to influence their perceptions of how we pay.

Employees do not think about pay all the time. It becomes a sensitive issue in the workplace when something happens to make the employee believe that his or her standard of fairness is being violated. As employers, we have the opportunity to create the ground rules for fairness. We also have the opportunity to violate the rules by acting contrary to our policies and philosophy. Following the rules we make helps us retain the employees we want to keep.

When Pay Practices Are Confidential, Do We "Walk Our Talk"?

When pay is supposed to be private we spend a great deal of effort in managing it. We try to make differences in pay related to differences in contribution. At the same time, if we have been operating for several years, we are probably paying employees for their length of service, even though that is not part of our compensation philosophy or in our mission statement. Does this help to retain employees?

Sometimes, Pay Is Public

We know what elected officials are paid; their salaries are public information. We know what the top executives of public corporations are paid, or at least what they were paid the previous year; we can find that information in proxy statements. Salaries of professional athletes are public, as are the amounts that entertainment figures are paid for a particular project—a film, TV episode, or recording.

Some pay practices make pay public. Pay for jobs covered by collective bargaining agreements is public; wages are listed in the contract. Pay for jobs with narrow bands and step increases is essentially public. Pay of employees of public institutions such as state colleges is also public, although not easily accessible.

Incentives

> "What will you do to retain me?"
> "I will give you financial incentives."

As we have seen, money as a motivational tool has real limits in complex organizations. However, money can be an effective motivator under some circumstances. It can be a powerful method of retaining employees when we use it narrowly, selectively, and for short-term goals. We can use it to retain specific employees for specific purposes for specific periods of time. We can do that through well-designed financial incentive plans. Such plans feature:

▶ Financial incentives that are significant to employees and too large for other organizations to easily "buy out."

▶ Goals that employees can have a reasonable expectation of achieving and that are visibly linked to the employees' performance.

What We Pay for When We Use Incentives

Incentives are a method of distributing pay. If we think of paying for different types of performance with different forms of pay, then

---

Risk and Reward

Whenever we pay an incentive we may ask ourselves the question: Would the employee have stayed and worked so hard on the project if we did not have the incentive? The only answer is that neither we nor the employee knows for sure. As people responsible for results, we have to consider the alternatives, weigh all the costs and apply our best judgment.

---

incentives fit in with base pay, merit increases, and gainsharing as just one way of matching compensation to performance.

It could be argued that incentives have an advantage over most other pay practices. In an incentive plan, if the goal is not achieved the money is not paid. As a regular practice we hire employees and give promotional increases in the hope that performance will match the pay.

Incentive Plan Design—Overview

Incentive plans are stated as "if-then." If you achieve the objective then you will get a reward. It is this conditional form that gives us the ability to retain employees while we receive the benefit of their contribution.

Bonuses Are Different from Incentives

Bonuses are an extra. You do not have to achieve anything in order to receive one. For example:

► Our organization has a good year and decides to give each employee a bonus of 2% of salary. The definition of a "good year" may be as simple as having the money to pay a bonus. The bonus goes to whoever is on our payroll when we pay it.
► Last year we lost money and did not pay merit increases. Now, six months later, we appear to have turned a corner and we give all employees a $400 bonus to help morale.

Many organizations, including nonprofits, have annual incentive plans. They are built on the operational objectives of the business plan. Typical goals are related to: customer service, safety, market penetration, turnaround time, quality, or cost cutting. The usual potential payout is less than 5% of salary. Annual incentive plans are a useful part of the overall pay strategy, but the payout is too low to retain employees.

Two types of cash incentives that do have the potential to retain employees are:

1. *Project completion incentives.* If you stay eight months, through the end of the project, we will give you $5000.
2. *Stock options.* We will give you options on 1000 shares of our stock. If we prosper, the options will be worth a lot of money.

Here are overviews of these two methods and how they work.

Project Completion Incentives

The advantage of project incentives is that we can target the employees we want to retain. Unlike our overall compensation philosophy, flextime, and training, which are available to everyone, project incentives are tailored to the employees and the circumstances. Usually, the incentive is for a dollar amount to be paid at a certain date. Employees have reasonable expectations of reaching the goal and earning the bonus. For example, we need three employees with specific skills to start a new distribution center. We give each of them an incentive to stay: "If you stay with us for 13 months to complete the project, we will pay you $10,000."

The design of project completion plans is simple: If the employee stays with the project for the stipulated period, then he or she gets the predetermined bonus.

At the end of 13 months we may not care if the employees continue with us. Their skills may still be desirable, but not critical to our success. Or, once the project is complete, there is no work left for the employees and we want them to leave. Another example: We want employees to stay with us through a merger. At the end, their jobs will go away. See Figure 11.1 for more examples.

Figure 11.1   Examples of project completion incentives.

▶ We are going through a merger and want to keep our customer service representatives on the job for the next six months. We fear that they may leave because they anticipate that their jobs are going away. We offer them an incentive of 15% of pay if they stay for six months.

▶ The manager of a department took a job with a competitor. We are concerned that she will hire several of her old staff members for her new organization. We offer a 20% bonus for anyone who stays for nine months.

▶ We are putting in a new computer application. It is a two-year project, critical to our success. We need a team in place for the duration. Our project has milestones at approximately six-month intervals. We pay incentives of 10%, 15%, 20%, and 30% of pay at each milestone, if we make each goal. Smaller payouts are made if the project is running late.

▶ The Y2K problem has led to the widespread use of financial incentives in many organizations. We have a critical problem and there is a tight labor market for people with the skills to fix it. Those who do have Y2K skills are in a strong bargaining position.

How big does the bonus have to be? The terms of the twenty-first century employment relationship cause us to throw out the old guidelines. It used to be that we offered bonuses of 10%, and they usually worked. Now there are no rules. We need to consider:

▶ Motivations of individual employees.

▶ Current market for their skills.

▶ Length of time needed.

▶ Value to us of retaining employees and the impact if we do not.

If there is a group of employees that we wish to retain, then we go with the probability that a 15% to 20% bonus will work.

Today's Employees Have More Choices

Here's the dilemma:

> I'll get a 15% payout if I stay in my current job for the next six months. Another company will pay me a salary that is 10% higher than my current one and give me an additional 5% to sign on. That new job is interesting and it is a good company.

Three possible responses:

1. I'll stay; there are more opportunities here.
2. I seem to be very marketable. I think I'll wait until we get toward the end of this project and look for a new job then. I'll try to set it up so I have some time off in between.
3. I'll take the offer if they add an extra week of vacation.

If there are specific employees in unique situations, we have another way of finding the right amount. We can turn the question that we started with ("What will you do to retain me?") around and ask: "Given our objective, what can I do to retain you?"

Stock Options

Stock options can make employees rich. Or, they may be worth nothing. Once limited to senior management, stock options are offered to more and more employees, and in some organizations to all employees.

An option is a right to buy a stock at a specific price, the exercise price. By itself, an option has no value. Options gain value when the market price exceeds the exercise price. If the business does well, the market for the stock grows. Employees can exercise their options to buy the stock, and then sell it at a profit. They receive the difference between the market price and the exercise price. Employees usually have to be on the payroll when they exercise their options. So, stock options retain employees who see the reasonable possibility that the stock price will rise, enabling them to sell the stock and make money.

Anything to do with stock is inherently risky. Risk factors include:

▶ *Market.* Will there be a market for the stock?

▶ *Market price.* Will the price be substantially above the exercise price?

▶ *Time.* How long must the employee stay with the business to see a real gain?

We read about businesses whose options provided phenomenal payouts and employees became millionaires. Does the phrase "Silicon Valley millionaire" come to mind? We do not hear about all of the companies that do poorly and go out of business, leaving the stock options worthless. There are few press releases announcing failures.

Stock options are useful in retaining employees in start-ups for

---

Employees' Views of Stock Options

"We have a fantastic product. We could be the next Microsoft and I'll make a ton of money."

"The money isn't all that great, but if the thing works my options will more than make up for it."

"I'm tired of waiting. Maybe there will be a payout from the options but for now there's nothing. I'm leaving for another company where I will get paid a lot better."

"Sooner or later the stock market will go up and I'll cash in."

"I was glad to be one of the few employees to receive options. They must like what I do. I think I'll stick around for a while."

"It was all right to live on hopes and promises when I was single and it was just me. Now I have a family to support and I need more money coming in regularly."

"The market was good last fall. I should have cashed my options. Now the market price is below the exercise price and the options are worthless."

a limited period of time. They can be offered to all employees to encourage teamwork and focus everyone's attention on the goal. We can vary the number of options according to the employee's contribution. Some young companies use options to replace a portion of a salary because the options require no dollar outlays.

Options play a different role in retention in larger, established businesses. Here, options are part of the overall pay strategy. They are a way of distributing pay based on the success of the company in the stock market. There is less risk in the stock of an established company and therefore less reward compared to a start-up. Options can be granted selectively to the individual employees we want to retain. They send the message "You are important to us and we want you to stay" more clearly than a financial payout does.

Appreciation

"What will you do to retain me?"
"I will show my appreciation for your contributions
to our organization."

Employees leave their employers because they do not feel appreciated. In the survey research for this book, 24% of the respondents checked that they left their last job because of being "Not valued for my contribution" and/or "Unappreciated."

Appreciation is not related to money, flexible work hours, or career opportunities. It is more personal. When we express appreciation we recognize an individual employee's unique contribution. It is a way of saying:

"I observed what you did."

"It has value."

"My telling you that I observed what you did and that what you did has value demonstrates my respect for you and forms a connection between us."

We do expect employees to show initiative, teamwork, creativity, and other skills. After all, we select employees on the basis of

---

What Happens When We Show Appreciation

"It's nice to know that someone is paying attention."

"Chris always seems so demanding. When she says that I did a good job it really means something."

"It's nice when your coworkers say thanks."

"She noticed."

"I am not saying that it makes all those long hours worthwhile, but it helps."

"He sent me a note of the telephone call from the customer thanking me for what I had done. And, *he* thanked me, too. It's nice to know that I am appreciated."

"I thought that Dave was so wrapped up in what he was doing that he couldn't see how much he depended on others. I am glad that I was wrong."

"After the presentation the big boss came up to thank me. He has never done that before. I guess it was good."

---

their abilities in those areas. But we do not want to take those skills for granted. We isolate employees and create an impersonal workplace when we do not recognize their contributions. No matter how internally motivated an employee is, or how high up the ladder, hearing that one's contribution is recognized and has value is important.

Recognizing and Appreciating

Saying "thank you" is the first and best way of expressing appreciation. It is most effective when we say it as soon as we are aware of what a coworker did.

Sometimes, though, we want to do more. We may want to give a tangible reward. And we would like to give the award in a way that shows we understand what the recipient values. For example:

Juanita comes to you and says, "I have been thinking about the long lines we have at our registers. I know that customers get annoyed with the wait. Why don't we ask some of the people in the office to help out? It would give them a chance to see our customers, instead of just knowing them as accounts. Here is a plan of how it would work."

Joe stays late for three nights to help you on a presentation you are doing for the board because your staff member who was supposed to work on it just quit.

We recognize that Juanita's initiative and Joe's willingness to pitch in are above and beyond their typical role and we are appreciative. We thank them for their contributions. We also want to give them something tangible. Money comes to mind, but then we have second thoughts:

▶ *Value.* How much is it really worth? If we give them too little will they be insulted? If we give too much are we overpaying?

▶ *Equity.* Have other employees done something equally significant in the past and were not recognized?

▶ *Jealousy.* If we do not recognize everyone who had a part, the ones we omit may be jealous and could cause trouble.

▶ *Finances.* Money is tight, and we are already paying them salaries and benefits.

▶ *Favoritism.* Our motives might be suspect.

▶ *Anomaly.* Juanita has poor attendance; can we give an award to someone who is not reliable?

▶ *Precedent.* How will we recognize similar actions in the future?

▶ *Appropriateness.* Do we have to do anything? Although their actions were outside their job descriptions, we do not expect those to limit responsibility.

By the time we work through our doubts several days have passed. We can no longer give an "immediate" award. We are not sure if we should give any award. Our initial desire to recognize exceptional contributions is entangled with undesirable side effects. Rewarding employees is not easy.

The Problem with Money

Money sends a special message, but it may not be the one we want. Cash awards can cause dissatisfaction and disaffection. Giving money to show appreciation says:

"I value what you did."

"I value it at X dollars."

We do not want to put a price tag on Juanita's and Joe's contributions. We still want to give them an award. It just will not be in the form of cash.

Demonstrating Appreciation

Here are three methods to recognize contributions without being entangled with money:

1. Spirit awards—given by any employee to recognize and reward desired behaviors.
2. Discretionary awards—given by supervisors to recognize and reward desired behaviors.
3. Rewards programs—organizational recognition.

These three programs are also useful in retaining volunteers. We can recognize and show appreciation to those who make special contributions, whether it is the number of hours they invest with us, their reliability, a willingness to show up at the last minute to fill a need, or their good humor in the face of difficulties.

Spirit Awards

Spirit awards are noncompetitive. We can give them out every time we want to express appreciation. We can visibly show that

---

What Happens When Employees Recognize and Show Appreciation to Each Other

"Bob gave me an award ribbon for helping him on his project. He didn't have to do that, but it was nice to get it."

"I have been trying for weeks to get Ann to understand how we fill out the A-71 form. She finally got it. She gave me an award ribbon to thank me. I am glad she recognized the effort I put into it."

"The manager saw me helping that old guy who was returning a sweater. It took a long time for me to explain how returns worked and what we needed from him to give him a credit on his account. The manager gave me an award mug. He said that he appreciated my patience with customers. It's good to know that the managers understand when we have to work extra hard to do our job."

"I had to clean the file room and wasn't looking forward to it. I mentioned it to Greg and he said he would help. He did a really good job, encouraging me when it seemed like we still had a lot to do. I gave him a spirit award. I was glad to give him recognition for helping out."

---

appreciation with tokens such as ribbons, pictures, mugs, pens, paperweights, cards, or similar items that can be kept on walls or desks. Tokens are simple reminders that something special has occurred. We want them to be visible and talked about. They express appreciation and show others that a coworker has done something of value for us. Any employee can give an award and recognize a coworker, even one's boss. To make it easy and convenient for employees to participate we can give each employee a supply of awards to distribute.

Introducing spirit awards may sound easy. It should be effortless to express appreciation. It may be, but it is hard to do in an environment where showing appreciation has not been valued. As in other areas when we want to make a change in the behavior of all employees, we have to start at the top with senior management taking the lead. The people at the top have to show that it is okay to visibly appreciate employees. To make a spirit award program successful, senior management has to show that:

> "Yes, we expect you to be creative, show initiative, and exhibit teamwork, every day in your job. We also want you to know that we appreciate it when you do so."

Senior management can demonstrate that message by giving awards to peers. This says that the spirit awards are not just for the lower-level employees; they are for everyone.

Communication.   Ongoing discussion in staff meetings, newsletters, posters, or e-mail about the value of recognizing contributions keeps spirit awards visible. Publishing the names of recipients in the newsletter or other organization-wide medium reinforces the message.

Discretionary Awards

Sometimes we want to give additional recognition. For example:

- ► We know that Juanita is a fan of our local football team. We can give her two tickets to a game.
- ► When Joe stayed late for three nights he was not able to have dinner with his family. We know that family is important to him. We give Joe a $75 voucher he can use at his favorite restaurant.

The significance of these awards is that we demonstrate that we know something about the employee as a person. The message is both:

"I appreciate what you did."

"I recognize what you personally value."

We can give discretionary awards in addition to spirit awards. Joe and Juanita can receive the public recognition of the ribbon or coffee mug as well as the personal recognition. Like spirit awards, discretionary awards are noncompetitive. Giving an award to one employee does not preclude us from giving it to others. We can give discretionary awards at all levels of the organization. A $75 certificate may not be considered a significant award for an employee earning $75,000 a year. A book, a bottle of wine, a golf umbrella, or other items that reflect an understanding of the individual's interests are more appropriate. If we have little money we can limit the awards to $5 or $10 dollars. A greeting card with a personal message is significant.

Communication. We want to tell others what Joe and Juanita did and that we are rewarding them. It might be at a staff meeting. There we can use it as an opportunity to strengthen our commitment to recognizing employees who demonstrate our organizational values.

Rewards Programs

Sometimes we want organization-wide recognition of special contributions. Or, we want to recognize employees who regularly demonstrate particularly high levels of customer service or other values. This can lead to an "employee of the month" and other more formal programs. They are formal because they require:

▶ Criteria—what we want the award to represent.

▶ Nominations—a method to identify potential winners.

▶ Selection—the need to review the nominations and screen them against the criteria.

They are also exclusive. Although we can award 12 employees over the course of a year, we can recognize only one employee per month. Because of the exclusiveness we want to be sure that the awards are viewed positively. Figure 11.2 shows guidelines for implementation.

Communication. Award winners deserve visibility throughout the organization. Organizations with little money to spend on awards can feature winners in association with regular operational activities such as including their pictures in brochures and

Figure 11.2   Guidelines for "Employee of the Month" and similar awards.

> ▶ Reason for awards—to promote excellence? signify our values? show the spirit of our organization?
>
> ▶ What will be rewarded—demonstrating initiative? handling emergencies? eliminating waste?
>
> ▶ Boundaries of the group—entire organization? team? business unit?
>
> ▶ Recipients—individuals only? teams? work groups?
>
> ▶ Eligibility requirements, if any—length of service? levels in the organization? attendance?
>
> ▶ Eligibility for awards, if any—once per year? never again? not again for the same reason?
>
> ▶ Nomination process—anyone can nominate? supervisors can nominate a member of the staff? self-nomination?
>
> ▶ Selection—vote of all employees or volunteers? supervisor? special committee?
>
> ▶ Administrative responsibility—supervisor? director of finance? human resources employee?
>
> ▶ Award—picture on the wall? lunch with an executive? day off with pay?
>
> ▶ Communicating results—small party? cookies by the coffee machine? newsletter?
>
> ▶ Criteria for maintaining the award program—number of nominees? feedback? lack of controversy?

asking them to introduce speakers at meetings. Figure 11.3 has a short list of no- and low-cost awards. Figure 11.4 has an example of an awards program.

Making Appreciation Successful in Retaining Employees

The employees we want to retain are taking actions and demonstrating behaviors we want to recognize. Building connections with

Figure 11.3   Examples of no- and low-cost awards.

- ▶ Thank-you letter.
- ▶ Gift tied to a hobby.
- ▶ Lunch with top executive.
- ▶ Three-day weekend.
- ▶ Featured in publications.
- ▶ Day off on birthday.
- ▶ Trophy.
- ▶ Contribution to an organization that the person honored supports.
- ▶ Tickets to game or concert.
- ▶ Presenter at a company function.
- ▶ Inclusion on a high-visibility team.
- ▶ Training course for a new skill.
- ▶ Catalog gift certificate.
- ▶ Gift certificate for dinner or videos.
- ▶ Opportunity to introduce speaker at fund-raiser.
- ▶ Flowers.
- ▶ Car washes.
- ▶ Parking space.
- ▶ Sandwich in the cafeteria named after employee.
- ▶ Name on plaque in reception area.
- ▶ T-shirt.
- ▶ Tickets to luncheons sponsored by business organization.
- ▶ Seats in the organization's box at a sporting event.
- ▶ Conductor of tour for visitors.
- ▶ Pizza party in employee's honor.
- ▶ Picnic cooler.
- ▶ Represent organization when it receives an award.
- ▶ Letter of thanks from president to employee's family.

Figure 11.4   An organization awards program.

January 18, 2000

To: All Employees

From: Pat Anderson (president)

Introducing **SWIFTY**—Our New Award Program

New Reward Program	I am pleased to announce that the board of directors has approved a new plan to reward employees who go above and beyond their jobs. The board recognizes that your commitment and your actions have made it possible for us to increase our ability to serve customers. The **SWIFTY** program honors employees who demonstrate those responses.
What Is Rewarded	There are two categories of **SWIFTY** rewards:

▶ **Suggestions** for improvements in operations—what should be done, how it can be done, how we will know if it is an improvement.

▶ **Results** from taking on work that goes beyond the job—special projects, handling emergencies, dealing with the unexpected, and similar actions.

Forms for each category are attached.

Eligibility	All employees except executive team members are eligible.
Nomination Process	Any employee may nominate another employee, or you may nominate yourself. A nomination may be for an individual employee or for a team.
The Reward	Each **SWIFTY** award consists of a **SWIFTY** pin and lunch with the chief executive officer. A copy of the letter announcing the award will be placed in the recipient's personnel file.
Decision Making	The **SWIFTY** team will meet once a month to review nominations and make recommendations to me. There is no limit to the number of awards given each month.
Administration	**SWIFTY** was developed by an employee team based on focus groups of a cross section of employees. That team will administer the program for the first year and evaluate the results.

Figure 11.4   *(Continued)*

SWIFTY Award Application for Suggestions

Description of suggestion:

What do we need to do to implement it?

How will we know if it is an improvement?

- -

Other information attached (at least one of these must be included):

___ Plan of action.   ___ Budget.

___ Cost/benefit analysis.   _____ (Other).

Name of employee(s) or employee team submitting this suggestion:

_____

Telephone number of contact person: _____ Date: ___/___/___

_____

SWIFTY Team Action

Dates: Received ___/___/___   Discussed ___/___/___

Recommendation made ___/___/___

Recommendation: Award   ___ Yes   ___ No

Final disposition: Award   ___ Yes   ___ No   Notify nominators ___/___/___

(Continued)

Figure 11.4   *(Continued)*

SWIFTY Award Application for Results

What results should be recognized?

Which employee(s) did this?

Why is this important to us?

- -

Employee(s) or employee team nominated:

_____

Employee(s) or employee team making this nomination:

_____

Telephone: _____   Date: ___/___/___/

SWIFTY Team Action

Dates: Received ___/___/___   Discussed ___/___/___

Recommendation made ___/___/___

Recommendation: Award   ___ Yes   ___ No

Final disposition: Award   ___ Yes   ___ No   Notify nominators ___/___/___

them by telling them that we see what they are doing and know it is valuable creates reasons for them to stay with us. If visibly demonstrating appreciation is a new way of behaving in the organization, we need a program to get it started. It may sound strange that a formal mechanism is required to express appreciation. Sometimes we need help to get over the hurdle of doing something different.

Getting senior management involved was discussed under spirit awards. Two other actions we can take to make it easier to show appreciation are:

1. Give the program a name. Naming a program gives us an easy way to refer to it. We can call it the Spirit of (our company name) or name it after our logo or current CEO or location or anything that associates it with the organization.

2. Be attentive to cultural differences. Some employees may be uncomfortable about being in the spotlight; public recognition may be distressing. Be watchful for signs of that and show appreciation in ways that recognize the behaviors while respecting individual differences.

Benefits

"What will you do to retain me?"
"I will give you good benefits."

We spend a lot of money on our major benefits such as healthcare, retirement, life and disability insurance, and vacation and sick time. Does that expenditure help us retain the employees we want to keep?

We know that benefits matter. The "Survey of Factors Influencing Employees to Stay With or Leave Their Employers" (Chapter 18) found that benefits are a critical factor in attracting and retaining employees. "Benefits" was the:

▶ Top attractor with 57% of the respondents checking it as a reason to stay with their current employer.

▶ Second highest preventer with 38%.

▶ Tenth highest reason, out of 44, for leaving the previous job, at 16%.

These responses are not age-related. The responses on attractors were similar for the under age 25 group and the 55 to 64 group. The same pattern held for preventers and for reasons for leaving the previous employer.

Benefits Are Personal and Private

The money we spend on organization-wide benefits programs is unrelated to an employee's job and performance. The employee with heavy healthcare expenses may be at the upper end of the normal distribution curve of our employee population shown in Figure 4.1 in Chapter 4, in the middle, or at the bottom. We cannot pick and choose who receives specific benefits. Anything we do with benefits affects everyone.

We want to attract and retain employees with our benefits programs. At the same time we may suspect that we retain some employees because they are afraid of losing benefits. Those employees

---

What Employees Say about Benefits

"Everybody seems to offer the same things. When one employer improves healthcare then everyone else does it, too."

"I don't care about benefits. My spouse has medical coverage."

"I need healthcare for my kids. As a single parent that is really important. I won't take a job that doesn't offer good coverage."

"I want the money and a good 401(k). I'll take care of everything else myself."

"I negotiated an extra week of vacation when I agreed to come here."

"I took advantage of the cafeteria plan. I was able to get the full healthcare coverage I want."

"The 403(b) is good here. I enjoy my job, but at some point I will leave. This way I can take the savings with me."

stay with us out of a fear that another organization may not be as generous as we are. Even if the next organization has equivalent benefits there may be a waiting period, during which time employees are either without coverage or have to pay for their coverage themselves. The survey on retention supports that theory.

Using Benefits to Attract Employees

Benefits cannot help us retain only the employees we want to keep. But we need to be competitive with our benefits when we recruit employees. We are unlikely to attract employees because we have many more choices in healthcare coverage or offer more life insurance than the competition. But, we will dissuade employees from coming to work for us if our benefits are significantly less than the competition's.

Communicating Benefits

Employees value their benefits, but they may not realize all that we provide for them. We give employees booklets and forms when they first come to work for us and additional information as we make changes. Employees often think that benefits are complicated and give up reading about them until they have a specific need or want to file a claim.

One way to remind employees what we offer is to distribute annual, personalized benefits statements. Typically these list each benefit, accompanied by a brief description and reference to more information. We can also show our cost for the benefit. That can include individualized amounts for Social Security, retirement, and other pay-sensitive benefits, and average costs for healthcare and similar benefits.

Offering competitive benefits and administering them well is one way to show that we value and respect employees. Chapter 13 on the work environment has more to say on the importance of that message in retaining employees.

12

Development and Career Opportunity

"What will you do to retain me?"
"I will give you opportunities to develop and use new skills."

The twenty-first century employment relationship has redefined development and career opportunity. In the old employment relationship:

"Development" was classroom training to gain technical skills required by the job.
"Career opportunity" was moving up the hierarchy.

The new definitions are:

"Development" is gaining new skills, taking advantage of many different methods of learning, that benefit employees as well as the organization.

Employees benefit by experiencing greater satisfaction about their ability to achieve results on the job and by taking responsibility for their career.

The organization benefits by having employees with more skills who are more productive.

The words "career" and "opportunity" are no longer tied together. "Career" means moving around in an organization and between organizations as well as up. "Opportunity" means the chance to learn new skills. Job offers are evaluated from the perspective of their contribution to the employees' learning and future employability rather than the status of the job in the organization's hierarchy.

Survey Data

Employees tell us that the availability of skill development opportunities and career movement are key attractions. That came through clearly in the research conducted for this book. The top three reasons for leaving the last job were:

"Lack of career opportunities"—1st place, 32%.

"No opportunity to move up"—2d place, 29%.

"Dead-end job"—3d place, 25%.

When we look at the reasons employees are attracted to their employer we see:

"Career opportunities"—7th place, 45%.

"Skills development opportunities"—12th place, 36%.

Barriers

Both we and our employees find great value in providing development and career opportunities. However, it may be hard to put into practice. Some of the reasons are:

▶ *Focus on the immediate.* It is not always easy to pay attention to development when we put all of our energies into meeting customer demands. Development is an investment—it pays

The Argument for Organizations to Stay Out of Employee Development

Organizations do need skilled employees. In a time of global interdependencies and technological change, our jobs change and the skills needed to perform them also change rapidly. Organizations use their resources most effectively by buying the skills we need when we need them. When we no longer need the skill then we discard it and buy new skills. We welcome the possibility that our employees develop the new skills we need but it is up to them to do so. This is especially true now that there is more parity in the employment relationship. We hire employees with the skills we need, and pay them. Employees provide skills in return for that pay. We expect employees to take responsibility for their own development so they can maintain their employability. We are happy to have them continue to work for us in new areas using their new skills. Besides, if we invest in employees' development, they can take their skills with them and we lose our investment.

off in the long term. Getting products and services to our customers is urgent and can be all-consuming.

► *No payoff for us.* We also may fear that the amount of money, time, and effort we put into employee development will pay off for someone else. We will invest in development and lose it when employees take their skills elsewhere.

► *Hard to manage.* We depend on individual supervisors to provide opportunities for their employees. They are not all equally interested or capable of doing that. Some employees might get more support than others.

► *Misuse of lateral moves.* Employers who use them to transfer underperformers taint the idea of lateral moves for skilled employees.

► *Question of who has the responsibility.* There is also disagreement in how far organizations should go to develop employees, and how much employees should do it on their own.

The Argument for Organizations to Actively Help Employees Develop Skills

Organizations do need skilled employees. In a time of global inter-dependencies and technological change, our jobs change and the skills needed to perform them also change rapidly. That is primarily for technical skills, though. There are other skills that we need in our employees—management skills such as decision making, communication, customer service, attention to quality, leadership, and so on. These core skills are needed in all of our jobs. We need employees who can apply their skills in a way that helps us achieve our objectives. When we hire, if we have a choice between two candidates, one with slightly better technical skills and the other with slightly better management skills, we will choose the latter. Management skills are harder to develop.

We hire employees who want to learn. We believe we must invest in our employees by providing opportunities for them to develop their skills and exciting job opportunities so they can find careers with us. We understand that employees may develop their skills here and leave. We are convinced that providing opportunities helps us recruit and retain the people we want. That pays off for us in the long run.

► *To Go Further*

Davis et al., *Successful Manager's Handbook.*
Waterman, Waterman, and Collard, "Toward a Career Resilient Workforce."

See the Bibliography for citations.

Development in Organizations

Organizations benefit when they actively support development and career opportunities. They benefit from both the increased ability to achieve results and the ability to retain the employees they wish to keep.

Figure 12.1 illustrates a model of development that leads to those outcomes. It has five phases:

1. Assess skills:

   Gather feedback from multiple sources.

2. Analyze:

   Combine data, analyze, and evaluate.
   Identify impact on the organization of further development of skills.
   Consider employee's interests.
   Consider opportunities to utilize skills.
   Choose two or three skills to plan to develop initially.

3. Plan:

   Describe the selected skills as behaviors.
   Tell what the employee will be able to do when the skills are developed.

Figure 12.1   Model of development in organizations.

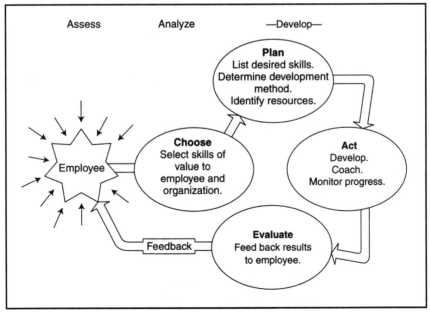

Decide on activities that will develop those skills.
Identify the resources needed, including money, time, and a coach.
Set a time frame for each skill.
Determine how progress will be monitored.

4. Act:

Implement planned development.
Coach.
Monitor progress.

5. Evaluate progress:

Feed back to employee for next assessment.

The process concludes when the employee develops new skills that meet the original objectives. It then loops back to a new assessment.

Continuing with Development and Career Opportunities

The next four sections describe tools that support development, career opportunities, and retention.

DEVELOPMENT

▶ Feedback—letting employees know how well they are doing.

▶ Nontraditional development—alternatives to classroom learning.

CAREER OPPORTUNITIES

▶ Job posting—moving around the organization.

▶ Dual career ladder—opportunities to use technical expertise and be rewarded for it.

Feedback

"What will you do to retain me?"
"I will give you feedback so you will know how you are doing."

Employees get feedback all the time. Carol is told that she does a good job of keeping the work group stocked with supplies. Robert is told, "You do good work." Or Joan does not hear any comments after she makes a major error in a report for a customer. All of those are examples of feedback, but they may be received differently than we intended. Carol might think, "She tells me that I keep us in supplies. Good. But she doesn't say anything about the way I deal with difficult customers, which is my job and much harder." Robert appreciates hearing that he does good work and has no idea of what is good about it. Joan may think that the error was insignificant because her boss never commented on it. Each of these is a form of feedback, but is it effective? Does it help employees improve performance? Does it really tell them what they want and need to hear?

Employees taking charge of their careers want feedback. They want feedback on results. Equally or even more important, they want feedback on their skills. Employees cannot change what has happened, but they can change their skills to produce better results in the future. It is this latter, *developmental* type of feedback that employees seek.

To be effective as a retention tool, feedback must be:

1. *Relevant to the job.* Carol's primary function is to work with customers, and ordering stock is merely a small extra task that she takes on.

2. *Specific, not global.* Robert needed to know exactly what was good about his performance.

3. *Timely.* Waiting six months for Joan's performance rating to tell her that she did a poor job is not useful for her development and works against her supervisor as well.

Giving Feedback

Giving feedback is hard to do. We often feel uncomfortable doing it. That is especially true when there is a skill deficiency. Telling Joan that she made a big mistake in a report for a customer, almost causing us to lose the account, is not easy. We are angry when it happens but do not want to express that anger directly. So we

wait. Then Joan prepares a highly detailed and thoroughly re-
searched report for another customer and we do not want to refer
back to the earlier poor work. We also neglect to tell her that the
more recent report was highly detailed and thoroughly re-
searched.

Two more examples:

We do not give feedback when something is not working well.

It happens all the time. An employee gives us inaccurate information. We think, "Well, it just happened once. It is not a pattern. He
knows that it was wrong. I do not need to say anything to him."
A week later it happens again. Now, we begin to wonder if he
does know how to do it right. Maybe there is a problem. Again
we dismiss it. It happens a third time and now we want to take
steps. We pull Brad aside and tell him that the data is wrong because he made incorrect assumptions and he is going to have to
do a better job of finding the correct information. And, we add,
this is the third time that it has happened! Brad says, "I didn't
know it was wrong! Why didn't you tell me? I thought I had the
right sources." A problem that could have been fixed two weeks
ago has lingered, the employee is angry because he did not know
he was doing something wrong, and we have lived with the bad
information.

We often do not give feedback when an employee does something well.

Robert does good work. We expect it of him and he does consistently well. He has just completed a project and his customer calls
us to compliment Robert. Robert understood the requirements,
the customer reports, suggested creative ways of handling difficulties, and delivered on time. Robert always returned calls and
e-mail promptly. The customer is pleased with Robert and with
the project.

We start to write an e-mail passing the compliment on to Robert,
and to our boss. Then we get a call on another matter. Now we decide to go over and tell Robert personally. But he is not there. We go
back to the e-mail but now something else happens, and we have to
leave. We tell ourselves that we will mention the compliment to
Robert. By the time we do so we have forgotten the details and tell
Robert, "You do good work."

Feedback Tools

If we believe that it is important to give effective feedback, then it helps to acquire a habit of doing so, just as we do for anything that we find difficult but know is necessary. Here is a method to help you get started. It has three parts: an agreement, a checklist, and a list of suggestions.

The first part is an agreement which spells out the roles and responsibilities for employee and supervisor in giving and receiving feedback.

SUPERVISOR	EMPLOYEE
Describes the behaviors expected.	Demonstrates understanding of the behaviors expected.
Tracks employee behaviors.	Keeps notes of own behaviors.
Meets with employee regularly to discuss skills and their impact on work.	Appears at meetings prepared to discuss own skills and work.
Focuses on skills and performance, not on the person.	Listens to comments without becoming defensive.
Passes on observations from others, after having assessed them.	
Tells employee promptly when he or she demonstrates a skill at a high level (or fails to do so when the impact is substantial).	

The second part is a checklist of the behaviors that you expect to observe. It is easier to give feedback if you know what you are looking for. Here is a sample based on the administrative assistant job description in Chapter 6. It shows the first skill, with its behaviors. Either the employee or supervisor or both can complete it.

Feedback on Skills of Administrative Assistant

Place a check mark if the behavior is present and a zero if it is not.

Administrative Skills   Performing everyday tasks in an organized and efficient manner; managing time and information to ensure that information flows appropriately and that priorities are met.

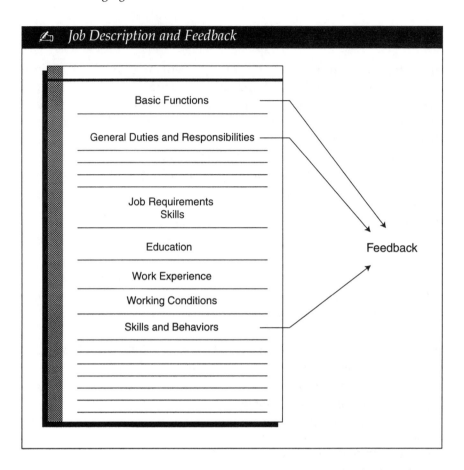

The employee:

1. ___ Examines procedures to identify aspects that can be improved.

2. ___ Applies policies and procedures that affect the job.

3. ___ Understands how the work of other departments affects one's own work.

4. ___ Obtains the resources needed to do own job.

5. ___ Sets priorities for one's own work.

6. ___ Prepares concise, informative, and timely reports for others.

7. ___ Organizes materials within own work area.

8. ___ Identifies resources to perform work when not available.

9. ___ Prepares descriptions of key tasks so that others may perform them.

10. ___ Develops a method of sharing information with others.

We can get more information if we add a rating scale—for example, a scale of 1 to 4 where:

4 = Consistently exhibits the behavior.

3 = Most of the time exhibits the behavior.

2 = Some of the time exhibits the behavior.

1 = Rarely exhibits the behavior.

This technique can be adapted to combine employee and supervisor ratings to achieve a consensus. The format in the box has columns for the employee's rating, the supervisor's rating, and a rating that both agree on. The "Agree" column is based on a discussion between them which can be very valuable as the two compare and interpret observations of behaviors.

The third part consists of suggestions on developing a habit of giving feedback:

▶ Write a note to yourself whenever you have a strong reaction to an employee's behavior. Include the situation, the behavior, and the reason for the strong reaction. A word or two for each is enough. This is a reminder for yourself, not a report to others.

▶ If the action is exceptionally praiseworthy, tell the employee. The quicker you do it, the better for you and the employee. Think of the employee as a customer to whom you must convey information.

▶ If the action shows an exceptional deficiency that must not recur, tell the employee immediately, *if you can do it without anger*. If you are too angry, wait and discuss it the next day.

▶ Keep the notes for your regularly scheduled meeting.

Administrative Skills Performing everyday tasks in an organized and efficient manner; managing time and information to ensure that information flows appropriately and that priorities are met.

| | RATING | | |
EMPLOYEE BEHAVIOR	EMPLOYEE	SUPERVISOR	AGREE
1. Examines procedures to identify aspects that can be improved.	____	____	____
2. Applies policies and procedures that affect the job.	____	____	____
3. Understands how the work of other departments affects one's own work.	____	____	____
4. Obtains the resources needed to do own job.	____	____	____
5. Sets priorities for one's own work.	____	____	____
6. Prepares concise, informative, and timely reports for others.	____	____	____
7. Organizes materials within own work area.	____	____	____
8. Identifies resources to perform work when not available.	____	____	____
9. Prepares descriptions of key tasks so that others may perform them.	____	____	____
10. Develops a method of sharing information with others.	____	____	____

Feedback for Generation X

Feedback may be particularly important for Generation X employees. They grew up with computers, a technology that tells them immediately whether they are doing something right, or not. If you misspell a word, it is highlighted on the screen. If you make an error, the program does not run. You are continually shown how well you are doing. Generation X employees may be looking for the same kind of quick response from the boss.

360° Feedback

The method of gathering feedback just described is informal and can be done between any employee and supervisor. It can be tailored to the individual employee and supervisor's style and relationship. It does not depend on any organization-wide support system. Organizations may introduce more formal methods of gathering information and giving and receiving feedback. One that is widely used is *360° feedback*. In 360° feedback, employees receive feedback from the different people with whom they interact. This includes:

▶ Peers.

▶ Subordinates.

▶ Supervisor.

▶ Customers.

▶ Suppliers.

Key steps in an organization's 360° feedback program are:

▶ Prepare questionnaire—standard for the entire organization or individualized by job description.

▶ Identify the respondents—names offered by employees or computer-generated.

▶ Distribute surveys—by mail or e-mail, or distributed by employees to their respondents.

▶ Compile returns—track and enter responses.

▶ Provide reports to employees—format, analyze, and summarize.

The data can be collected, compiled, and analyzed using scanned documents, interactive voice response units, or on-line forms.

Nontraditional Development

"What will you do to retain me?"
"I will give you many methods of developing new skills."

From our organization's perspective, we want development to serve a purpose for us and our employee. That requires planning. We have to state what we are going to do, how we will do it, and what we will observe at the end. We need to identify and allocate resources, including money and time and someone to coach the employee, to help him or her keep on track. This is a lot more complicated than it used to be.

Figure 12.2 shows a sample plan.

Development can work only when it is a cooperative arrangement between employee and supervisor.

EMPLOYEE	SUPERVISOR
Commits to develop skills that benefit the organization.	Commits to support the employee by allocating resources and giving feedback.
Monitors progress.	Monitors progress.
Evaluates results.	Evaluates results.

There are many different ways of learning. The traditional classroom training linked to the job requirements can still be an effective method of developing skills. Some of us learn best when we have an instructor to answer our questions and coach us over difficult material. For some material, class discussion is the most effective teaching method. Pages 139 to 143 describe other learning methods with examples of their use.

Figure 12.2 Sample development plan.

Development Plan for ___Pat Smith, Administrative Assistant___ as of ___May 1, 2000___

DEVELOPMENTAL AREAS	PLANNED ACTIONS	DEMONSTRATED RESULTS
Provide information so that others can perform Pat's work when she is away from her desk, even if it is just for a short time.	Prepare a desk description that lists key activities and location of files (physical and computer) and flow of work in key projects.	Customer contact reps and supervisor are able to generate reports and otherwise access information in Pat's absence. Complete in three months.
Pat needs to understand how her own work relates to providing service to customers.	Focus on selected assignments. Ask Pat to identify sources of requests and where the results go. Discuss with Pat what happens when the tasks are not completed as expected. Prompt Pat to consider the cost and the impact on customer service when tasks are not completed. Encourage Pat to ask questions if not sure of impact.	Get feedback from a sample of reps monthly. They should perceive that Pat's skills have improved.
Pat needs to understand what has priority to customers, and why.		

(Continued)

Figure 12.2 *(Continued)*

Step 1: Identify the skills to be developed. Consider the skills that have the greatest impact on job performance. They may be:

▲ Skills in which employee is already strong but additional development can have a substantial impact.
▲ Skills that are relatively weak and need improvement.
▲ Skills that can be developed fairly quickly.
▲ Skills that are newly required for the job.

Step 2: Determine one or more ways to develop the skill. In addition to classroom training or conferences consider:

▲ Books, articles, videos, especially those with tests of the subject matter.
▲ College course work.
▲ Computer-based training.
▲ Formal education.
▲ Job share.
▲ Joining a professional association.
▲ Mentoring from a supervisor or another employee who is expert.
▲ Networking with other employees with similar interests.
▲ On-the-job learning.
▲ Programmed learning books.
▲ Simulations and games.
▲ Special assignment.

Step 3: Evaluate progress. Find a way to answer the question: How will I know if my skills are increasing?

Filling In for a Supervisor

Supervisors take vacations, are ill and away from work for several weeks, or leave. Someone has to be responsible for operations. The supervisor's boss or a peer could temporarily replace him or her. Or the supervisor's absence can be used as an opportunity for a staff member to *preview* the role of supervisor and develop supervisory skills such as delegation, coordination of work, monitoring performance, and leadership, as well as communication, analysis, organization, and planning.

For short-term absences, responsibility for running day-to-day operations can be rotated among the staff. The acting supervisor should be expected to maintain standard records, coach others, and represent the unit at staff meetings. The developmental experience can be evaluated with feedback from the regular supervisor or the boss and a self-assessment by the acting supervisor.

Employees' development plans can be used to select an acting supervisor for a long-term need. The acting supervisor will get involved with a broad range of leadership responsibilities and the regular supervisor's performance expectations and job description can be adapted. Select one or two skills to focus on and negotiate a method of evaluation based on those skills.

Job Shadowing

An employee can learn by spending time observing and performing some of the tasks of an employee who regularly does them. A plan that describes what the learner should look for and how one knows what one has learned turns this into a developmental opportunity. Learning about the job of an internal customer or an internal supplier can broaden an employee's view of the continuum of work he or she is a part of. The experience can develop skills related to analysis, initiative, quality assurance, and customer service.

Purchasing and accounts payable employees work with the same customers but from different angles. Gary from purchasing can shadow Ann from accounts payable and gain a broader picture of the flow of transactions and a better understanding of customer requirements.

Many organizations have both office and field operations. The office receives requests for services and the field executes the orders. There can be tension between the two based on lack of understanding of how the other works and the stresses faced. Job shadowing gives each firsthand information on the other's job. Besides fostering individual development, this can have a positive impact on overall relations between the two areas.

Job Rotation

This is a step beyond job shadowing. Employees use their skills in a new area and develop new skills, responding to the requirements of the positions. Job rotation can be part of a formal program or a temporary opportunity to move into a different job.

New college graduates often start their employment in management development programs. They move through three to five areas before assuming greater responsibilities. The same concept can also be used for current employees.

An extended absence can be an opportunity for a temporary swap. Employees usually fill in for each other under those circumstances. The move is developmental when the work is assigned with deliberate attention to growth and employees are asked to report on and evaluate what they learned.

Mentoring

In a mentoring relationship, an experienced person guides a less experienced one. The guidance may include information and advice on the current job or help with career movement. It is a personal rather than a supervisor-employee relationship and may continue for many years. It gives the less experienced person an opportunity to test ideas and express opinions in a safe environment. Originally, mentoring was spontaneous, growing out of the personalities of the two people. Today's organizations often create mentoring programs and encourage the creation of those personal relationships.

Phil is moving from staff to supervision and knows that it is a difficult transition. He is assigned a mentor, Alice, who helps by giving him a safe place to test his ideas about handling difficult staff members, planning, meeting budget targets, and other expectations of his new role.

This is also a developmental experience for Alice. She gains experience in coaching and communication.

Self-Paced Learning

Books that allowed people to learn and test their knowledge at their own pace have been available for years. That same idea—people working at their own pace and having the answers to test questions available—is now computerized, providing more possibilities for both learning and evaluation. Success depends on the ability to be self-motivated, since the learner does not receive step-by-step encouragement (at least not from another person).

Computer applications from word processing to network design are widely available on-line and on CD-ROM. Employees can chart their own path through them and select the skills they need for the job. There are evaluations at the end of each module that provide feedback as well as a measure of progress in learning the content.

Video- and audiotapes are useful in developing language skills. They show accurate accent, grammar, and inflection and allow an employee to compare his or her voice to the standard.

Task Force

Membership on a task force takes employees out of their everyday work and puts them in new roles with new expectations and responsibilities. Task forces provide opportunities to develop a broad range of skills.

Joyce is an expert systems analyst. She wants to increase her skills of communicating with customers and understanding their requirements. She can do this in a task force that assigns participants, in pairs, to gather information.

Tom wants to develop his leadership skills. Chairing a task force gives him the opportunity to learn to motivate employees who do not report to him, develop planning skills as he prepares and implements the timetable, and gain oral communication skills as he participates in meetings and in presenting the results to management.

Teaching

An employee who is already skilled can further develop that skill by becoming a coach or instructor or mentor to other employees. Teaching something you know so that others can learn it develops skills in structuring communications and adaptability to the learning styles and abilities of those being taught.

Roz has been asked to teach budgeting to new supervisors. To do that she learns to break a large process into modules, set objectives for each, and adapt her communication style to different learners.

Human resources introduces a new performance management system. Supervisors are trained to deliver the program to their peers and to employees throughout the organization. Those instructors develop skills in presentation, communication, and monitoring performance.

Volunteer Service

Learning related to work can take place off the job. Employees already participate in volunteer activities, from coaching basketball to serving on city councils. These activities often provide more opportunity to learn certain skills than their current jobs afford. The development plan describes the responsibilities of the volunteer job, what can be learned that is applicable to the regular job, and a method of determining progress in development.

Sam, a customer service representative, is a member of his community's school board. In that role he has to review reports and discern key points. He has to listen to others and present reasoned arguments to gain support on issues he champions. He may ask questions to gather information and identify new sources of information. All of these skills are applicable to his job.

Sam's development plan can include growth in any of these areas.

Barbara, a frontline supervisor, is the secretary to the board of trustees at her church. She participates in formulating and monitoring the budget, analyzing the facilities and planning for future needs, and developing programs to attract new members. The leadership skills she acquires can be used on the job.

On-the-Job Learning

Development constantly takes place on the job. We are learning all the time. When we list on-the-job learning in the development plan we call attention to what already exists. More importantly, we also identify areas to emphasize and state ways to measure what has been developed.

- ▶ *Written communication.* The employee drafts communications for the coach to critique. The coach does not make corrections but helps the employee learn grammar and writing for specific audiences.

- ▶ *Initiative.* The employee makes a note of ideas for making changes to own work, volunteering for assignments, and asking questions on procedures. He or she reviews them with a coach, who encourages the employee to go forward with those ideas on the job.

What Is a Coach?

A coach is a resource in development as much as money, time, and material. A coach is someone who offers encouragement, cheers the employee on, and provides feedback. The supervisor may also be the coach. Other possibilities are a coworker, friend, spouse, relative, or another employee who wants to develop coaching skills.

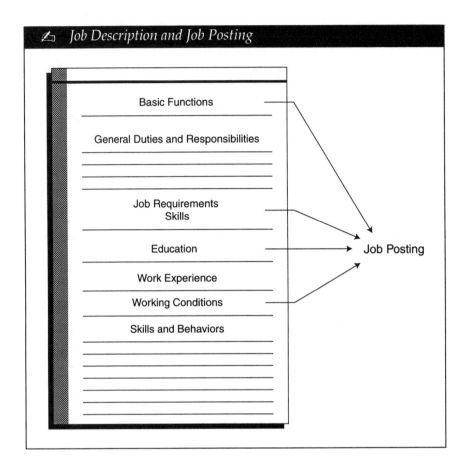

Job Description and Job Posting

Basic Functions

General Duties and Responsibilities

Job Requirements
Skills

Education

Work Experience

Working Conditions

Skills and Behaviors

Job Posting

Job Posting

"What will you do to retain me?"
"I will give you opportunities to compete for jobs within
the organization."

Job posting programs, found in many of today's organizations, are designed to:

▶ Provide management with a method for finding qualified employees.

▶ Give employees opportunities to make a job change.

An often overlooked result is that job postings give employees information on future careers. Job postings may be the single best method of communicating information on the jobs that exist within the organization. When we announce current openings we tell employees the overall responsibilities and important tasks of the position. We tell them the skills needed to perform the tasks. It is a way for employees to learn about the types of jobs we have as well as the skills required. Figure 12.3 is a sample announcement.

Job posting does not take the place of a career counseling and guidance function. If we do not have that function we can still tell employees about the work we do and the jobs we have through job posting. They then can:

▶ Learn more about the job by talking with the hiring department.

▶ Decide if it is work that they may want to do in the future.

▶ Take steps to develop the skills.

It is to our advantage to help supervisors find employees who have the skills to do the job. Similarly, it is to our advantage to provide a method for employees to take charge of their own careers and move around our organization, rather than another organization.

When a job posting process does not work, it is usually because of one of two factors:

1. The design of the job posting process.
2. The culture of the organization.

Job Posting Process

A well-designed job posting process puts supervisor and employee together. Here are five design criteria:

1. The posting advertisement:
   Reflects the job description.
   States how the position fits in the department and organization.
   Emphasizes skills.

Figure 12.3   Sample job posting, based on the Administrative Assistant job in Chapter 6.

Job Opportunity
Administrative Assistant, Customer Contact

Posting date: September 13, 1999

Job Summary

Serves our customers by supporting the work of the customer contact representatives (CCRs) and their work environment; maintains inventories of supplies and material required by the staff to perform their tasks and to provide service to customers; posts schedules and availability lists so CCRs can plan for coverage; prepares and processes all nonroutine correspondence and communications including advertising material, statistical reports, scheduling, and personnel changes; coordinates communication among customers, suppliers, and staff regarding products and services.

Requirements for the Position

▶ Education: Two to three years of course work beyond high school in accounting, business, or related field or equivalent work experience.

▶ Work experience: Two or more years in providing administrative support to an operation.

▶ Skills:

Administrative.
Analysis/problem solving.
Attention to detail.
Communication.
Organization culture and knowledge.
Technical.

Physical Demands

▶ Typical administrative office conditions.

Working Conditions

▶ Normal business hours.

Figure 12.3 *(Continued)*

To Apply

Applications due in Human Resources: September 20, 1999.
List your current job, education, and work experience.
For each of the skills, give an example of how you have demonstrated that skill in situations similar to those described in the job summary.

Selection process: Interviews with supervisor and team members.

Timetable: Interviews the week of September 20, with a decision expected by October 1.

Limits the stated requirements to those factors that are truly
required.
Describes working conditions.
Tells selection process.

2. Information should be distributed promptly and widely. Instead of limiting the announcement to one location, we can ask ourselves, "Where are the employees who have the skills to do this work?" With electronic methods we can send the advertisement to every possible site at the same time so that all employees have the same opportunity to respond and the same time frame to do it in.

3. The time frames should be published and adhered to. We should meet employees' expectations as to when they will be scheduled for interviewing and testing and when and how they will learn about their status.

4. Employees applying for positions should describe on their application the skills they have that meet the requirements. Employees may decide not to post when they see for themselves that they lack those skills at present.

5. Employees who are not chosen should receive feedback. An employee wants to know what job-related skills need to be developed. An employee also wants to know if interviewing skills need improvement.

Organizational Barriers

As we improve the job posting process, we can begin to identify ways in which the culture interferes with its effectiveness. Here are eight statements to help identify barriers. Going through the list quickly and entering the first reaction is a good way of getting immediate perceptions down on paper. Asking employees to respond to these same questions gives us a chance to see how management's actions are perceived. See Chapter 20, "Employee Satisfaction Survey," for more about surveying employees.

QUESTION	YES	NO
1. We give credit for knowledge of the organization when we make selection decisions.	____	____
2. Employees can start new careers internally without having their pay reduced substantially.	____	____
3. We announce and celebrate lateral moves to the same extent we do promotions.	____	____
4. We look at management skills as much as technical skills for most jobs.	____	____
5. Employees who take risks by moving to a new position may be considered for their old position if the new one does not work out and the old one is still open.	____	____
6. Our employees say that in getting selected what you know is more important than who you know.	____	____
7. We do not routinely transfer employees who have poor performance.	____	____
8. Our experience shows that employees regularly move across departmental and divisional lines.	____	____

If the response to more than half of the items is "no," the organization has probably put up barriers to using job posting for career

> **Employees See Barriers to Changing Jobs through Job Posting Process**
>
> "I got my degree with the help of tuition assistance and now I don't get a chance to use my skills here."
>
> "They bring in consultants to do the interesting work and leave us with the maintenance stuff."
>
> "That department would rather hire someone from outside than take an employee from another department."
>
> "The job postings are all show. They find a way to say that everyone from the inside is not qualified."
>
> "I want to change careers, but I can't seem to do it here. There is such a prejudice against people who are willing to start from the bottom in a new area."

movement and retention. Employees may not believe that the system provides real opportunities, so they will leave.

"Promoting" Internal Movement

Changing the barriers to internal movement is hard, but the cost of not changing may be high. What is our investment in employees who leave? What does it cost to replace the employees who leave because they did not see a future for themselves with the organization? Refer back to Chapter 4 for a method of examining those costs. Cost data gets attention, and can be used to build a persuasive case that the organization will be more successful when support is provided for employees to grow and prosper within it.

Dual Career Ladder

"What will you do to retain me?"
"I will give you opportunities to be rewarded for what you want to do and do well rather than for what you do not want to do."

We have both supervisors and experts in our organizations. Supervisors take responsibility for functions and people. Experts analyze data, serve customers, plan projects, design processes, and maintain equipment. The contributions of the two roles are different and so are their skills. Traditionally, we valued supervisors more than experts, as evidenced by the distribution of rewards and recognition. Supervisors got more money, bigger offices, better equipment, more privacy, and increased visibility to top executives. Going up the ladder meant moving from a technical or professional role into management. It "forced" people into management.

An Example of a Bad Move

Thomas is a brilliant engineer. Six months ago he accepted a promotion to head our specialty products engineering team and now he and the unit are in trouble. Productivity is low. Two of our top engineers quit, telling us that they were frustrated working for Thomas. He does not know how to delegate and they found themselves with less authority than they had under the previous manager. Before he was promoted Thomas went through the assessment process we use for all managerial positions. Thomas did okay—not great, but okay. He wanted the position and we thought that his technical skills would make up for his weakness in managerial skills. It was a bad decision for both Thomas and us.

Thomas now believes that he should have stayed in a staff position. But he had wanted the recognition, the extra pay, and the opportunity to be heard at the upper levels of our organization. Managers get those things; engineers, no matter how brilliant, do not. We want to move Thomas to a staff position. He is not sure he wants to stay as manager but he does not want to give up the access to information and visibility he has as manager. A recruiter calls Thomas with an offer for a senior engineer position in an organization that has a dual career ladder. It gives engineers the same visibility and recognition it provides managers. Thomas accepts their offer and makes a graceful exit. We are left with a job to fill, and without a brilliant engineer.

> ### Overpromotion
>
> Do you remember the Peter Principle? In his 1969 book of that title, Laurence J. Peter wrote about the tendency to promote people to the "level of their incompetency." George is an accountant. He receives a promotion and does very well. He receives another promotion, with the same result. At some point George is promoted beyond his ability to perform. It is most likely to happen when George is promoted to manager

Does "forced" sound too strong? There were —and are—a lot of pressures on employees to move into management when opportunities arise.

▶ We offered employees those positions because we thought that the best performers could supervise. After all, they knew the work, didn't they?

▶ Employees took supervisory positions partly because of the rewards and partly because supervising provided an opportunity to do something different. They did what was expected, not because they necessarily wanted to do the job or had the skills to do it well.

▶ Other employees also expected the top performer, or the one with the most seniority, to move to supervisor. If anyone else became the supervisor, that person's competence to do the job was questioned.

▶ Supervisors have a possibility of continuing to move up in the organization, earning more rewards. Experts, on the other hand, can go only so far; there is a limit to the grades and the rewards they can earn.

Keeping Our Expertise

This process of moving our best performers into supervision also forces employees out of the organization. Our best clerical, technical, and professional employees who enjoy their work and do not want to supervise will leave us and go to another organization where they can continue to do what they want to do. We need a method of keeping them in the work they do best.

Ladders That Fork

We often speak of climbing the ladder in our organization. The standard image is a single ladder that starts in the mail room and leads to the president's office. But there are other ways to move through our organizations. Today, when employees want to move *around* the organization as well as *up,* we have to change our picture. A dual career ladder is one alternative to the single ladder. It is particularly effective in providing upward mobility and increased responsibility to experts.

Organizations that have a large number of employees in a clerical, technical, or professional group may already have career paths for levels below the first level of supervision. Dual career ladders extend those paths upward. Experts and supervisors share the same grades, or bands, and the same potential for rewards.

When there are few employees in a clerical, technical, or professional group, we do not usually construct dual career ladders. Nevertheless, there are times when we need expertise more than we need supervisors. Or we have employees who do not make good supervisors but whose expertise we need to retain. We can keep the concept of dual career ladders and allow them to receive the rewards and recognition that we give to supervisors but enable them to use their expertise.

In a dual career ladder, employees moving up in their career see a fork in the road. One path leads to supervision and the other to higher levels of clerical, technical, and professional expertise. We benefit in two ways:

► Productivity—Employees perform well at what they do best.

► Retention—Employees stay with us because they can do what they want to do.

Figure 12.4 shows a dual career ladder with three levels of career growth plus two levels of either supervisory positions or increasing expertise.

RUNGS ON THE LADDER

▶ *Entry.* This is the usual way of beginning on the career ladder. In an engineering career ladder, this is a starting place for new college graduates. In hospitals, the graduates of medical technology programs begin here. The entry level of a customer service career ladder is for employees with the right skills who will be trained on our systems.

Figure 12.4   Dual career ladder.

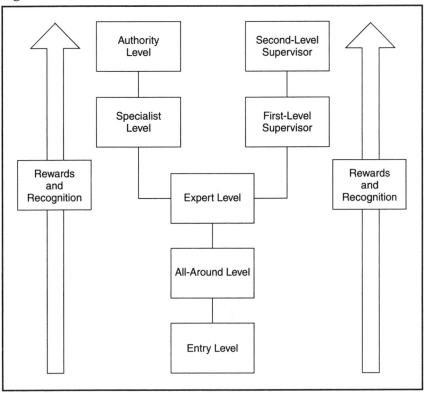

▶ *All-Around.* Employees with the skills to handle all of the regular, recurrent tasks with little supervision are here. Another term for this level is *journeyman.*

▶ *Expert.* Employees who are experts have the skills to handle all aspects of the work, including dealing with unusual and special cases. Other employees go to them for advice.

▶ *Specialist.* Employees at this level have in-depth knowledge of specialized aspects of the field. They are regularly called upon by others in the organization, both within and outside the field of expertise, for advice.

▶ *Authority.* Some employees are recognized as authorities by people outside the organization. They may publish in the appropriate magazines or journals, speak at conferences, and, in general, receive public recognition for their expertise.

Dual career ladders are particularly useful in flatter organizations where there are fewer ways to move up. With broader spans of control there are fewer supervisory positions. We encourage employees to consider opportunities to move around the organization and broaden their skills. Dual career ladders also recognize that there are times when we need expertise.

Making a Dual Career Ladder Work

There are prerequisites for making dual career ladders work within an organization:

▶ Definitions of the skills desired and results expected at each level of the career ladder.

▶ A true (not merely perceived) need for high-level technical or professional skills.

▶ Ability to address practical problems of reporting relationships. Some organizations consider the high-level professionals to be gurus. They are off by themselves and anyone who needs their expertise goes to see them. Essentially they are outside the organization. Most of us cannot afford to have that expertise unconnected with our operations.

▶ We also want to tell all of our employees about dual career ladders. In doing so we communicate a message that expertise is recognized, and we are signaling to employees, "You can be recognized for your skills without having to leave them behind and move into management."

13

Work Environment

Do these phrases appear in your vision statement?

"We value our employees."

"We treat each other with respect."

"We work together as a team to achieve results."

They do appear in the official statements of many organizations. They often reflect something real about our work environment. We do value our employees and their contributions. We do believe that managers should respect employees and that employees should respect each other. We do believe that working in teams will provide better service to our customers. The question is: How well are we doing?

How Well Are We Doing?

One way to find out is to ask our employees. We can conduct an employee opinion survey and ask, "On a scale of 1 to 5, where 5 is the highest, to what extent do you agree with the statement, 'Our organization values employees'?" We know that there are always some disgruntled employees but expect that most employees feel they are treated with respect. We would like to see 90% of our employees rate us 4 or 5. If you have surveyed your employees with a question like this, you probably saw results lower than that. Even employees who seem committed to their work and recognized and rewarded for their results may have rated us below a 4.

Why do we get these results?

Is it possible that we do *not* value employees and treat them with respect? There are, in fact, some organizations that do not treat employees very well. Employees are shouted at and demeaned. Employees are harassed. Employees believe management lies to them. Sometimes the problem may occur in an isolated part of the workplace. Sometimes particular groups of employees (such as women, minorities, people with disabilities, gays, or older employees) are targeted. Other times it appears that there is a culture that pushes all employees to behave badly toward each other. There is enough litigation to conclude that there are real problems in some workplaces.

The more likely reason for low scores is that the words "value" and "respect" are abstract. We all see them differently. How does management demonstrate that we value our employees? What do we do? What do employees observe? What does respect look like? Teamwork may be desirable, but do we in fact work in teams? As in other circumstances when we use abstractions, we may fail to communicate. Members of management have different ideas of what value and respect mean. And when we ask employees, they give those words their own interpretations.

Compare Your Own Results over Time

There is no easy way to compare the results of one organization with those of another. Each survey has a different set of questions and is conducted with different methods and for different purposes. The best comparison is within the organization over time. If you do a survey now and another one a year from now, with the same questions and methodology, you can track your own performance.

Responding to Surveys

When we ask employees to what extent they agree with the statement, "Our organization values employees," we give them a wide area to reflect on as they consider their response. The range includes:

▶ Pay.
▶ Distribution of work.
▶ Whether the supervisor says "hello" to everyone the first thing each morning.
▶ How quickly an employee in another area responds to a request.
▶ Selections for a task force.
▶ Whether the HMO pays for a particular procedure.

Defining What We Mean by "Value" and "Respect"

We can help both ourselves and our employees when we translate our abstract words into behavioral statements. That gives us and our employees a common understanding of what we mean. We help management by describing the words and actions expected. And we tell employees how they can expect to be treated and how they are expected to treat coworkers. Here are examples of behavioral statements that illustrate how management shows it values and respects employees.

"I will tell you about events in the organization that affect you."

"I will listen to your suggestions."

"I will tell you why I disagree with you."

"I will provide you with the resources you need to perform the work assigned to you."

"I will consider mistakes that you make as opportunities for growth and development."

"I will tell you what I expect of you."

"I will listen to your concerns about my behavior without becoming defensive."

"I will ask you what developmental opportunities you wish to consider."

"I will recognize diverse points of view."

"I will help you set goals that you can achieve."

Do I Know It When I See It?

There is an argument for keeping our words as abstractions and not attempting to be explicit. This is often referred to as, "I'll know it when I see it." The reasoning is:

> If you tell me that you treat me with respect, I should be the judge of whether or not you do so. Furthermore, if you give me examples, you are limiting the meaning of the word.

The counter to that argument is:

> That works well in personal relations. But we are an organization. We want to provide an organization-wide way of working together. To do that we all have to share an understanding of what we want to achieve. Putting our words into behavioral terms enables all of us to work toward a common goal.

We also want employees to demonstrate that they value and respect coworkers, including supervisors as coworkers. Examples of those behavioral statements are:

"I will share information with you."

"I will consider the potential impact of what I do on you and your work."

"I will recognize your contributions."

"I will not interrupt you unnecessarily."

"I will assume responsibility for my actions."

"I will give you feedback when asked."

"I will ask you a question when I need clarification on what you say."

"I will respect your time."

"I will give you credit for ideas that you originate."

"I will follow through on my commitments to you."

Resurvey Employees

Once we tell employees what we mean by "value" and "respect," we can change our survey approach. Instead of asking employees to rate the statement, "Our organization values employees," we ask them to rate the behavioral statements. We ask, "On a scale of 1 to 5, where 5 is the highest, to what extent do you agree with the statement: 'My supervisor tells me about events in the organization that affect me'?" We use three or four of those statements in our survey to obtain an overall rating for respect. This gives us a better idea of how we are doing. It also points to our weak spots. For example, the rating may be high on supervisors giving information to employees and low on providing resources to do the job. See Chapter 20, "Employee Satisfaction Survey," for more on conducting surveys.

Our Treatment of Employees Relates to Retention

It seems obvious that the better employees believe they are treated, the more likely they are to want to stay with our organization. The survey conducted for this book supports that. Top attractors were, with their ranking and the percentage of employees checking the response:

"All-around good employer"—2d place, 54%.

"Coworkers are good"—4th place, 50%.

"Boss is good"—6th place, 46%.

Not being treated well causes employees to leave their employer. Reasons for leaving the previous job include, out of 44 possible items:

"Conflict with boss"—14th place, 10%.

"Harassed"—25th place, 6%.

"Conflict within work group"—30th place, 5%.

"Discrimination"—30th place (tie), 5%.

Respondents translated those items for themselves. We can only infer that "All-around good employer," "Coworkers are good," and "Boss is good" are associated with being treated with value and respect.

▶ **To Go Further**

Herman, *Keeping Good People.*
Kanter and Stein, *Life in Organizations.*
MacDonald and Sirianni, *Working in the Service Society.*
Whyte, *The Organization Man.*

See the Bibliography for citations.

Creating Our Desired Work Environment

Once we and our employees have the same understanding of what our work environment should be, we are able to move toward it. The next two sections describe:

▶ Creating policies that tell employees what to expect.

▶ The role of supervisors in making the policies work.

Policies

"What will you do to retain me?"
"I will prepare and implement policies that facilitate your work
and do not put barriers in your way."

When we recruit potential employees, they want to know about our culture. Given their individual skills, career interests, personal life, and values, is our organization the best place for them at this time?

For example, we want to attract Don to a position at our help desk. We tell him about our mission and vision and what it is like to work in our organization. We tell Don that "we value and respect employees." We continue with descriptions of our compensation philosophy, opportunities for development, and flextime. We answer Don's questions with information about our policies.

Our policies match what Don is looking for and he accepts our offer. When Don begins working for us, will he find that our prac-

The Difference between What We Say and What We Do

OFFICIAL—LANGUAGE IN OUR POLICIES	ACTUAL—WHAT SUPERVISORS SAY TO THEIR EMPLOYEES
"We value all of our employees."	"Sorry, I don't have time to deal with this now. Catch me tomorrow."
"We pay for performance."	"Your rating is 7 on a 9-point scale. Great job. Your merit increase is 5% in this year's 5% program."
"Supervisors meet with their employees regularly to provide feedback on their work."	"I know I said I would meet with you now on that feedback form. But something has come up. Maybe we can get together after the holidays."
"Our selection process is based on what you know, not whom you know."	"I know you thought that you would get the promotion, but I had to accommodate the boss's protégé."
"Supervisors tell employees what is expected of them."	"I know we are in the second quarter already and you don't have your performance expectations. Why don't you tell me what you think they should be?"
"We understand that employees have a personal life. We have flextime to enable employees to adjust their schedules, with the agreement of the supervisor."	"If I let you come in later and stay later I'll have to do it for others."
"Supervisors encourage their staff to be creative and innovative."	"Why in the world did you . . . ?"

Why Do We Have Policies?

Maybe we can get around the difficulty of preparing policies by not having written policies at all. Some organizations believe that policies are unnecessary. They say that written policies interfere with their ability to change as circumstances change. These organizations say they have one policy: "To do whatever helps us grow our business." This can work in a new and small organization where the employees share a common set of values. Otherwise, it gives employees not one policy but a series of them. The policies derive from all of the communications received from members of management, subject to employees' various interpretations of management behavior. Each employee has a slightly different version, based on what he or she observed and inferred from the observation. On the whole, it is more straightforward to put policies in writing.

---

tices line up with our stated policies? Often we may say the right things in our policy statements, but they may be too ambitious or counter to our real culture or just plain too difficult to actually do. *We attract employees with what we say, but we can drive them out with what we do.*

We want our work environment to support and sustain employees. Just like our statements on how we value and respect employees, we do want to show that we understand how important employees are to our success. Sometimes we have difficulty in saying it.

One reason why it is difficult to write policies that align with our culture is that we have multiple cultures within our organization. Unless we are a young organization, we have a series of cultures built up under different leaders over a period of time. If our organization has been around for many years, we also have employees holding on to the old employment contract and thinking "entitlement" even as many employees embrace the new one. We want to retain many of the employees who wish the old contract was still tenable because we need their skills. At the same time, our policies have to reflect the realities of the new contract. What can we say? How do we write policies that we can confidently cite because we know that they:

▶ Represent our values.

▶ Can be implemented.

Writing Policies

We want policies to reflect our values and the kind of organization we want to be. One topic that many organizations grapple with today is personal use of computers, telephones, and similar office equipment.

> If we were living under the old contract we would probably forbid all personal use during business hours, or, at most, limit usage to one five-minute period a day. We expected employees to give us a good day's work for a good day's pay. Using our equipment for their personal use violated that norm. It also tied up the lines and interfered with business.
>
> Under the new contract we are less concerned with time and more concerned with results. However, we still do not want employees to tie up our equipment for extensive personal use during business hours.

Figure 13.1 is an example of how to formulate a policy that reflects our present values and accommodates our past ones. Figure 13.2 lists different ways to determine if our policy is practiced.

Employee Handbooks

Employee handbooks are the typical method of telling employees about our policies. Chapter 21, "Employee Handbook," describes the process of preparing one.

Practicing Our Policies

No matter what we say, as long as there is variability in our culture there will be variability in our practices. Two ways to reduce that variability are:

▶ *Policing.* Accounting, information technology, human resources, and other functions that are responsible for policies actively enforce them for consistent application.

Figure 13.1   Testing policies for consistency with valuing and respecting employees.

Situation   Employees use computers, telephones, pagers, radios, tape and video recorders, copiers, fax machines, printers, and other equipment to perform their tasks. The same equipment can be used for personal reasons. We want our policy on personal use to be consistent with our behaviors as well as our business needs.

Behaviors   Two of the behaviors listed earlier in this chapter as demonstrating value and respect are:

▶ Supervisor to employee—"I will provide you with the resources you need to perform the work assigned to you."

▶ Employee to employee—"I will assume responsibility for my actions."

Business needs:

▶ Equipment belongs to the business; it costs money to buy and maintain it.

▶ Equipment has to be available for business purposes.

▶ Users (employees) have to be available for business purposes.

Policy alternatives:

▶ Forbid all personal use.

▶ Forbid all personal use during business hours, and allow personal use during breaks, lunchtime, and after hours.

▶ Allow limited personal use, not specifying what we mean by "limited."

▶ Allow use for particular reasons; for example, parents can receive calls from their children.

▶ Limit personal use to certain hours of the day.

▶ Limit the length of time of personal use.

▶ Allow unlimited use.

Figure 13.1 *(Continued)*

> ► Allow each department or function to have its own policy, based on the business use of the equipment.
>
> ► Create different policies for exempt and nonexempt employees since we pay exempt employees for what they do and not for the hours they work.
>
> A possible policy:
>
> > We understand that the software on our computers is for business use only. Using it for nonbusiness purposes takes attention away from our ability to serve customers.
> >
> > We understand that the Internet, e-mail, and other tools are available for business purposes. Occasional personal use that does not interfere with our work or with the use of equipment for business purposes is acceptable.
> >
> > We do have the opportunity to use the software and other tools after business hours on our own time, to the extent that it does not impact our coworkers or operations.

► *Supervisory accountability.* Supervisors are already responsible for business results; since policies are meant to lead to results, let supervisors administer them.

If we expect our policies to exemplify what we mean by valuing and respecting employees, then leadership accountability meets that criterion and calling in the HR police does not.

Supervisors

"What will you do to retain me?"
"I will give you a supervisor who supports you in your work."

How many supervisors are there in your organization? A supervisor is anyone with employees reporting to him or her. Each one of these supervisors creates a unique work environment for employ-

Figure 13.2   Can we administer the policy?

Here are alternative methods to determine if a policy is being followed.

Computerized Monitoring

- ▶ Audit trails of computer and telephone usage.
- ▶ Use codes or keycards to control access to copiers and VCRs.
- ▶ Restrict access to certain Internet sites and area codes.
- ▶ Enable usage at set times.

Personal Monitoring

- ▶ Spot-check telephone usage by listening in.
- ▶ Have auditor walk around and view computer use.
- ▶ Have attended copy machines and VCRs.

Personal Responsibility — leave it up to individual employees.

Monitoring Job Performance — Supervisors monitor job performance and results, not how employee spends time.

Additional Questions to Consider

- ▶ Does one method work for all employees, or do we want different methods depending on:

    Employee access to equipment?
    Privacy of work space?
    Office versus field conditions?

- ▶ What degree of variability is acceptable?

    Do you want to treat all employees equivalently?
    Does rank have its privileges?
    Do employees who work under stressful physical conditions
       have more scope?
    Does it make a difference if employees work with external
       customers or internal customers?

The HR Police

I worked in an organization in which human resources employees reviewed every single performance appraisal. We looked for reliability in rating the results achieved against the results expected. If the supervisor gave a "meets goals" rating to an employee with 90% accuracy, did he or she give a higher rating to an employee with 88% accuracy? We could challenge supervisors and get them to change their ratings. We also could advise them if we thought that the results expected were too easy or difficult and suggest that they make changes for the following year. We were the HR police.

ees. There may be one set of policies, but if you have a dozen supervisors or a hundred or a thousand you have that many interpretations and that many local work environments. Conditions in each of those work environments either encourage employees to stay or give them reasons for leaving.

What Supervisors Do

We expect a lot from supervisors. We expect them to be both:

▶ Achievers of results.
▶ Leaders of people.

We expect supervisors to achieve results by leading others, and not by doing most of the work themselves. Supervisors are expected to plan the work, assemble and develop a staff, and coach that staff to perform the work. We may emphasize the importance of the leadership role by evaluating a supervisor's performance on input from staff. We may even decide to rate a supervisor's overall performance on a 50–50 basis: 50% on achieving business results and 50% on leadership.

In a large organization, a supervisor, especially a first-line

---

What Employees Want from Supervisors

► Feedback on how they are doing.
► Guidance and suggestions on dealing with difficult issues and people.
► Resources to do the work.
► Flexibility in hours of work.
► Recognition for a job well done.
► Salary reviews.
► Clear expectations.
► Training.
► Developmental opportunities.
► Chances to try new things.
► Opportunities to learn the business.
► Time to deal with personal issues.
► Fun.

---

supervisor, may have 20 to 30 or more employees to supervise. Levels of management have been eliminated as the organization "de-layered." In this environment, supervisors have to achieve results through their staff.

The situation in smaller organizations is different. Supervisors may have only two or three employees reporting to them. They have a functional workload in addition to their supervisory responsibilities. They are pulled between meeting operational responsibilities as best they can and attending to employees. The operational responsibilities have insistent deadlines and get their first attention. Setting expectations, working with employees to improve performance, providing development opportunities, retaining employees, even adding staff, can come in second.

Supervisors as Policy Administrators

We write policies to create a consistent work environment for our employees. Some of our policies are administrative: "Our work

---

Another Name for "Supervisor"

What's in a name? Here the word for a job with responsibility for achieving results through the work of others is "supervisor" with a small "s." "Supervisor" with a capital "S" is also a formal title, as are "Manager," "Director," and "Vice President." Some organizations use "Leader" as a title. Other new terms arise to reflect an organization's culture. Here we stay with "supervisor" with a small "s" to emphasize the relationship between the person with leadership responsibilities and his or her direct reports.

---

week begins at 12:01 A.M. Sunday and ends at midnight Saturday." Some are managed centrally: benefits, access to computers, providing references. Supervisors have responsibility for policies that require careful interpretation and are administered individually by supervisors across the organization.

All these actions create a distinct work environment for the employees they lead. As noted in Chapter 4, "As We Go Forward," supervisors have a key responsibility for retention. If you were the retention czar mentioned in that chapter, how would you prepare them for their task?

Preparing Supervisors to Retain Employees

Here are four actions to prepare supervisors to create a work environment that retains employees.

1. Define the job.
2. Select people with the skills.
3. Give supervisors the authority that goes with the expectations.
4. Train.

Role Models for New Supervisors

In some organizations there is the belief that frontline employees need more support, feedback, and recognition than supervisors do. The thought is that supervisors know what is expected of them and do not have to be praised for doing it. But new supervisors are like new employees. New employees learn the real culture of an organization by observing how others behave. Their role is new and they have a new set of behaviors to demonstrate. Their model is based on what they are most familiar with—the way supervisors have treated them and the treatment by their supervisor in the new position.

The type of support may change, but supervisors at all levels want to know what is expected of them and have someone tell them when they go off course. If they do not have support, then it is hard to provide it to others. It may not be their own boss who provides support; it may be a mentor or even someone outside the organization. But the boss has an especially important role in creating the work environment. It is difficult for supervisors to be supportive of their employees without receiving similar treatment from the boss.

Defining the Job

What are the responsibilities of supervisors? A short lists includes:

LINK EMPLOYEES TO THE BIG PICTURE

► Explain the organization's strategy and operations to employees.

► Tell employees how their unit's operations fit into and affect overall results.

► Communicate changes in policy.

PLAN AND IMPLEMENT WORK

► Manage a budget.

► Obtain resources.

▶ Forecast needs for resources.

▶ Reengineer the work.

▶ Improve quality.

▶ Develop measures.

▶ Create a safe work environment.

▶ Keep up-to-date on regulations affecting operations.

DEVELOP A STAFF

▶ Coach employees for performance.

▶ Provide feedback to employees.

▶ Maintain a work environment that is free of discrimination.

▶ Guide employee development.

▶ Select staff.

▶ Recognize performance.

▶ Build a team.

▶ Tell employees their expectations.

▶ Prepare job descriptions.

▶ Plan development and training.

▶ Hire.

▶ Fire.

▶ Recognize contributions.

▶ Recommend pay changes.

We expect a lot from a supervisor, more than any one person can actually do. For a supervisor to be successful, he or she has to have a defined role and expectations that are achievable. We can begin to describe the job of supervisor in our organization by focusing on what is particularly important for us and eliminating the rest.

As in Part II, "Foundations of Retention," we want an accurate description of what we are looking for before we try to find a person to do it.

What Else We Expect of Supervisors

Although they may not be in the job description, here are adjectives and nouns to describe how supervisors supervise.

ADJECTIVES	NOUNS
Accessible.	Champion.
Charismatic.	Coach.
Committed.	Diagnostician.
Courageous.	Enabler.
Knowledgeable.	Exemplar.
Paternalistic.	Expert.
Process-oriented.	Facilitator.
Trustworthy.	Listener.
Visionary.	Model.
Wise.	Planner.
	Risk taker.
	Steward.
	Strategist.
	Tactician.
	Taskmaster.
	Team builder.

Selecting People with the Skills

Chapter 8, "Retention Starts with Selection," shows how to take a job description and use it for selection. The same process applies to the selection of supervisors.

There is one special situation that may occur in filling a frontline supervisory position. We have an employee who is very skilled at the technical work but does not demonstrate the skills we want and need in a supervisor. (We can put her through an assessment center or other testing to determine her actual skill level.) The situation is complicated if we are a small organization. If we do not promote the top technical person she may leave. If we do promote her we can try, or hope, to develop her skills so that her behaviors do not cause others to leave. It is even harder if there is a general expectation that the job is hers.

Alternatives include:

▶ Reorganize and combine this function with another group under that supervisor.

▶ Reorganize, eliminate a level, and have the technical person and others in that function report one level up.

▶ Fill the position from outside with an employee who has the skills we want.

See the section on dual career ladders in Chapter 12, "Development and Career Opportunity," for another idea.

We can start to resolve our problem by talking with her. Does she really want to be a supervisor? Is she looking for a promotion? More responsibility? More money? She may be pleased that she has been asked for her input. She may offer suggestions that cut through the issues. Or, of course, she may be adamant about becoming a supervisor. We will not know unless we ask.

Giving Supervisors the Authority

While we ask our supervisors to be leaders of people and achievers of results, we often constrict their ability to take action. We give them a staff representing $100,000 in labor costs and equipment worth $50,000 and limit their spending authority for supplies to $100. We also limit their freedom to switch budget dollars from one category to another.

As we hold supervisors accountable for results we want to match their responsibilities with their authority. Here are some of the decisions that impact retention where supervisors often have limited authority or participation in decisions.

▶ External training.

▶ Internal training.

▶ $50 recognition award.

▶ Magazine subscriptions.

▶ Purchasing binders for a presentation.

▶ Lunch for the staff.

▶ Signs to make areas more accessible.

▶ Lawn mowing service to beautify the facility.

The individuals with the authority to approve those decisions may not realize the impact on retention. As retention czar, how do you manage this?

Training

Most of us are better at providing technical training than supervisor training. Yet, most organizations appear to devote more time and money to train employees to use computer applications than they do to develop supervisors. Training on the responsibilities for leading a staff includes these main topics:

▶ Selecting staff.

▶ Recognizing and rewarding contributions.

▶ Managing performance.

▶ Planning development.

▶ Identifying talent.

▶ Mentoring.

▶ Coaching.

▶ Building a team.

Spending Authority of Frontline Employees

We have increased the spending authority of frontline employees.

▶ We tell our billing representatives that they can resolve customer accounts up to $100.

▶ We tell employees on an assembly line that they can stop the line if they see a problem.

▶ We tell repair employees that they can order parts up to $500 without approval.

Do they have more autonomy than your supervisors do?

► *To Go Further*

Block, *Stewardship.*
Boyatzis, *The Competent Manager.*
Yukl, *Leadership in Organizations.*

See the Bibliography for citations.

► Modeling behavior.
► Managing conflict.
► Managing difficult employees.
► Administering discipline.
► Running a meeting.
► Demonstrating presentation skills.
► Delegating.

Rewarding Supervisors

So much of the success of our organization, including our ability to retain employees, depends on our supervisors. We need to keep their skills and requirements in mind as we develop policies and plan programs. They, more than anyone else, constitute the early warning system for employee retention.

14

Performance Management

"What will you do to retain me?"
"I will help you achieve results."

Job descriptions tell employees their responsibilities. They answer the employee's question, "What am I supposed to do?" Performance management answers the question posed by employee and supervisor together, "How will you and I know that the job is being performed well?" The use of the term "performance management" instead of "performance evaluation" or "performance appraisal" emphasizes achieving results, not rating an employee.

The employees we want to keep are looking to us for guidance. They want us to set goals so they will have a sense of direction for their work. They want someone to tell them when they are going in the wrong direction and provide a course correction when they make mistakes. Employees may be confident about taking charge of their careers. That is not the same as thinking they can do it without help. As discussed in "Feedback" in Chapter 12, many of our younger employees are accustomed to getting feedback and expect it.

Employees Want to Believe That the Work They Do Is Valued and Makes a Contribution

One of the responsibilities of an administrative assistant is to pay invoices. Paying invoices, by itself, is tedious and boring. But when paying invoices is seen as part of a larger purpose, then it no longer stands alone; it has meaning. Paying invoices is part of the process of obtaining resources for customer contact representatives so that they can work effectively with customers. Paying invoices also conserves our financial resources. Paying an invoice in time to take a discount saves money. Paying only for legitimate invoices saves money. Thinking of one's work in a larger context may not make a responsibility exciting. But now it has a purpose.

Sources of Difficulties in Managing Performance

Managing performance is an end in itself. It improves the ability of the organization to achieve results and be successful. But it is hard to do well. Employees and supervisor often experience it as subjective, superficial, and irritating. There is an annual form to complete. It always seems to be done in a rush. The words are vague—"Tim did a good job all year." Or the form has boxes for each of several skills or results. Supervisors check the appropriate boxes and no reason is given to Jane about why she received "3" in initiative instead of "4."

To complicate matters, the overall rating is often tied to our salary system. When we say to employees that "we pay for performance," the common understanding is that we give merit increases based on the overall rating of an employee's performance. Managing performance is hard enough. Linking the results to merit pay adds complications. Employees who are disappointed with the overall result, who feel that the rating is a surprise, who are unclear about what was expected of them, or who do not believe that they have been given the opportunity to correct problems, are unhappy with their rating. Basing increases on those results surely makes employees more unhappy and un-

> ### Do Employees Really Want Someone to Manage Their Performance?
>
> Each of us is an employee and can answer the question for ourself. Would it be a help or a hindrance to have:
>
> ► Expectations that tell you how your work impacts the bottom line, customers, or whatever is most relevant?
> ► A person you can comfortably go to for assistance and who won't hold it against you that you need help?
> ► Someone who will help you diagnose why you are having difficulties and offer training and development to prevent future difficulties?
> ► Clear signposts to tell you when you are on the correct path?

trusting of the organization's statement of paying for performance.

The employees we want to retain will not be unhappy with their ratings. They are valuable to us and their ratings will be high. They may be less happy with the "pay" part of "pay for performance." If we have a 4% merit program and actual increases range from 2% to 7%, there is not much differentiation in pay based on performance.

The combination of not managing, not evaluating, and not paying for performance makes employees cynical about the performance management process. The discrepancies may not be enough to make employees leave. But a better system may encourage them to stay.

Overview of a Performance Management Process

In the performance management process we:

► Set both quantitative and qualitative expectations.
► Monitor progress.
► Evaluate results.

Employees participate with their supervisors in every phase so that they:

▶ Understand their role in achieving results.
▶ Contribute suggestions on how to improve their performance.

Figure 14.1 shows the process.
Performance management looks at both quantitative and qualitative expectations and results.

▶ Quantitative expectations are based on the general duties and responsibilities in the job description.
▶ Qualitative expectations are based on core behaviors expected of all employees. The method of developing them will be discussed shortly.

Figure 14.1   Performance management cycle.

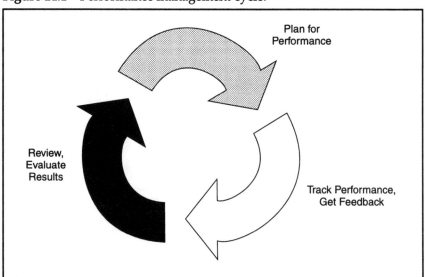

Both supervisors and employees have active roles in the three phases of performance management shown in Figure 14.1.

The description of performance management that follows is for a model process. Features include:

► Results expected linked to the organization's business objectives.

► Key responsibilities based on job descriptions.

► Measurable results expected.

► Employee participation throughout.

► Training for supervisors and employees.

The administrative assistant job description from Chapter 6 is used to illustrate the process.

Successful implementation of the model depends on having a culture that:

► Holds supervisors and all employees accountable for results.

► Supports training and development to give employees the skills they need to accomplish results.

Following the description of the model are suggestions of how to modify the process.

I. Planning Phase

This is the foundation for performance management. The supervisor and employee work together to set the *results expected* for the performance period. The results expected flow from the organization's goals and objectives and the employee's job responsibilities. When there is a shift in the employee's work assignment, it is appropriate to evaluate the performance to date and revise the results expected.

This phase ends with the completion of the results expected.

ROLES AND RESPONSIBILITIES

SUPERVISOR	EMPLOYEE
Helps the employee comprehend the link between the organization's goals and objectives and the employee's job responsibility.	Asks questions about the organization's goals and objectives.
Discusses how the employee's job responsibilities impact the goals and objectives of the organization.	Demonstrates an understanding of how the job responsibilities impact the ability of the organization to meet those goals and objectives.
Works with the employee to identify methods of measuring key responsibilities and determine results expected that are a challenge to the employee's abilities.	Suggests how to measure key responsibilities and the results that should be expected.

II. Throughout the Performance Period

Once the supervisor and employee determine their mutual expectations they work together on achieving those results. While the employee performs the tasks, the supervisor coaches and guides the employee in the performance of those tasks. And, together they collect examples of performance and track progress. Throughout this stage there are periodic conversations in which the employee receives feedback on that progress and has an opportunity to ask for coaching.

ROLES AND RESPONSIBILITIES

SUPERVISOR	EMPLOYEE
Observes, notes examples, and evaluates employee performance.	Collects examples of performance outcomes.
Tracks progress toward achieving results and shares information with the employee.	Tracks progress toward achieving results and shares information with the supervisor.
Coaches the employee and provides feedback on progress.	Seeks and accepts feedback on path toward achievement of expectations.
Identifies developmental needs that impact progress and discusses ways to provide that development.	Discusses development and training requests.

III. Performance Review

This marks the end of a performance cycle. It is a time to identify the *results achieved*, with examples, and give a *rating* to the achievement. Since performance management is a continuous process, the information from this phase becomes input to the next performance cycle.

ROLES AND RESPONSIBILITIES

SUPERVISOR	EMPLOYEE
Reviews the documentation he or she has maintained as well as the documentation provided by the employee and enters the results achieved. *Alternatively,* reviews the results achieved drafted by the employee.	Reviews his or her performance, drafts the results achieved, and provides documentation to the supervisor.
Rates each result achieved including the behavioral expectations.	Actively engages in the discussion of results achieved.
Completes the form and reviews it with the next level of supervision.	
Meets with the employee to discuss performance and ratings.	

Setting Quantitative Expectations

A model for determining employees' *quantitative* goals is:

▶ The board or council or governing body approves strategy.
▶ Senior management sets goals and timetables to implement the strategy.
▶ Supervisors develop plans to implement the goals and meet the timetables.
▶ Employees receive assignments with goals that will fulfill the plans.

Expectations are set at the beginning of the performance period.

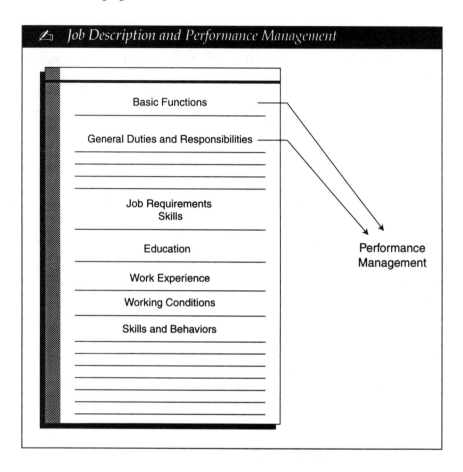

The responsibilities in the job description become the key responsibilities and results expected in performance management.

The supervisor and employee discuss how to measure the results expected and the targets.

Figure 14.2 shows how the job description becomes the basis for performance expectations.

Monitoring Performance

While they are setting expectations, the supervisor and employee plan how they will monitor progress. There are no surprises in performance management. Employees know how they are doing

Figure 14.2 Performance expectations for an Administrative Assistant.

The basic functions section of the administrative assistant job description begins, "Serves the external customers of XYZ Company by supporting the work of the customer contact representatives (CCRs) and their work environment."

The first key responsibility is taken directly from the job description.

The results expected, with the yardsticks and targets, are:

First key responsibility—Invoices: Process invoices; open and receipt invoices; verify transactions and amounts; prepare for payment; assign accounting and post invoices to appropriate accounts; maintain files of invoices; verify payment reports.

RESULTS EXPECTED	YARDSTICK	TARGET
All invoices are verified against packing slips or other documentation prior to approving for payment.	Source document listed on invoice.	No more than one invoice per month is missing a reference to the source document.
Invoices are sent to accounts payable so that the organization can take available discounts for prompt payment.	Accounts payable report.	No more than 2% of the invoices are sent late to accounts payable—excluding invoices with disputed items or other problems.
Invoices are posted to correct accounts.	Questions from employees responsible for the account.	No more than one misassigned account per month.
Copies of paid invoices are filed by account.	Invoices accessible whenever requested.	No more than five missing invoices per year.
Reports from accounts payable are reviewed to verify that (1) invoices have been paid and (2) no charges for other departments are charged to this department.	(1) Budget reports and (2) no inappropriate charges are discovered at a future time.	Resolves all instances in which another department's invoices are charged to ours.

Eliminating End-of-the-Year Surprises

When supervisor and employee discuss performance throughout the year, there are no surprises at the end. Employees know how well they are doing and have opportunities to improve. Employees know what they are measured on and where they stand.

---

throughout the year. If performance is lagging, then both supervisor and employee have the responsibility to:

▶ Spot it.

▶ Document it.

▶ Analyze why it is occurring.

▶ Take steps to prevent it from happening in the future.

Monthly or quarterly meetings are useful for ongoing monitoring but do not preclude additional sessions when needed.

Documenting Activities throughout the Year

Both supervisor and employees maintain documentation of actions and results throughout the year. These records provide a shared basis for understanding what has occurred. Keeping track of what happened throughout the year eliminates bias based on remembering only the achievements, or only the errors. It also prevents results from late in the year overshadowing results from earlier in the year. See Figure 14.3 for more about these and other rating errors.

At the end of the performance period we can describe the results achieved and rate them.

Results Achieved

The employee has enough information to prepare a draft of the results for discussion with the supervisor. Figure 14.4 shows the results achieved for the first key responsibility of the administrative assistant.

Figure 14.3   Typical rater errors.

We are all human and prone to make judgments in different ways based on different personal values and preferences. While there is no such thing as a perfectly objective system, we can improve our ability to be consistent when we are aware of our own potential for making errors. Here are some common performance rating errors.

Recall Accuracy
We differ in how well we are able to remember an employee's performance. Documentation is always helpful, but some actions do not lend themselves easily to documentation.

Our ability to recall is influenced by the timing of performance. We may remember the most recent occasions, for good or ill, better than those early in the performance period, or vice versa. We may remember performance that upper management commented on, again for good or ill, more than other performance.

Halo Effect
We may perceive an employee who does something well or poorly in one situation performing the same way in other situations. Or, we may perceive an employee who is popular or sociable performing better than an employee who is not so well liked or who is quieter.

Sometimes the past casts a shadow. Employees who perform well or poorly at one time may change and perform worse or better at a later time. We may carry the earlier impression to the new situation.

Categorizing
Sometimes we see the person and not the performance. We may stereotype by race or gender or religion or appearance. We then associate ability or behavior with a trait or characteristic. We may give more or less credit to the stereotype and give higher or lower ratings than the performance warrants.

A related error is to give more favorable ratings to those who are like us in an important area. The basis may be race or gender or religion or appearance. Or, the basis may be style—for example, a shared analytical approach to work.

Central Tendency
Some of us find it hard to make decisions on performance. We may be without documentation, lack confidence, or be fearful of the results of singling out an employee for praise or of confronting an employee who is rated lower than others. As a result, we give everyone the same rating.

Figure 14.4   Results against expectations for the first responsibility of the Administrative Assistant.

Key Responsibility 1: Process invoices; open and receipt invoices; verify transactions and amounts; prepare for payment; assign accounting and post invoices to appropriate accounts; maintain files of invoices; verify payment reports.

RESULTS EXPECTED	YARDSTICK AND TARGET	RESULTS ACHIEVED	RATING
All invoices are verified against packing slips or other documentation prior to approving for payment.	Source document listed on invoice. No more than one invoice per month is missing a reference to the source document.	Fifteen invoices did not include proper reference.	
Invoices are sent to accounts payable so that the organization can take available discounts for prompt payment.	Accounts payable report. No more than 2% of the invoices are sent late to accounts payable—excluding invoices with disputed items or other problems.	Fewer than 1% of the invoices were sent late to accounts payable.	
Invoices are posted to correct accounts.	Questions from employees responsible for the account. No more than one misassigned account per month.	Three invoices were inappropriately assigned to another area.	
Copies of paid invoices are filed by account.	Invoices accessible whenever requested. No more than five missing invoices per year.	After a problem with missing invoices during the first three months, introduced a new charge-out system that eliminated lost files. No missing files after May 1.	
Reports from accounts payable are reviewed to verify that (1) invoices have been paid and (2) no charges for other departments are charged to this department.	(1) Budget reports and (2) no inappropriate charges are discovered at a future time. Resolves all instances in which another department's invoices are charged to ours.	No outstanding issues.	

Figure 14.5 shows an example of a scale we can use if we want to give a rating to the results achieved. Descriptions of each level help bring consistency to a rating system used throughout the organization. There are no labels for the levels in this example. Labels often add confusion as we struggle to determine if "excellent" is higher or lower than "superior."

Figure 14.5   Descriptions of levels of performance.

---

4   Employee accomplished all aspects of the results expected in the key responsibility. Employee required little direction in day-to-day work but sought direction appropriately. Employee usually took the initiative in problem solving and problem prevention. This rating will often be earned by exceeding stretch goals or through successful response to extraordinary and/or unforeseeable circumstances.

3   Employee accomplished all aspects of the results expected in the key responsibility. Employee required little direction in day-to-day work but sought direction appropriately and took direction well. Employee often took the initiative in problem solving. There were few occasions that required the supervisor to intervene or redirect the employee's efforts. This level of performance can be achieved by employees who focus on their objectives and demonstrate commitment to our goals.

2   Employee accomplished most of the results expected in the key responsibility, but, at times, the supervisor had to intervene or monitor the employee's work. The actual accomplishment of the key responsibility required active supervisory involvement. The employee showed initiative in some of the activities required. This performance may be typical of an employee who is relatively new to the job or one who needs development in job content knowledge.

1   Employee accomplished little of the results expected in the key responsibility. Much of what was achieved required active intervention by the supervisor. The employee showed little initiative in taking responsibility for results. This performance may be typical of an employee who is a poor match for the job or requires development in problem solving, analysis, communication, or similar areas.

Qualitative Behaviors

Now we turn to qualitative behaviors, the core behaviors we expect from all employees. We begin with the behaviors that show how employees value and respect each other. To them we can add behaviors associated with the way we treat customers, demonstrate quality, and commit to personal development or other skills important to the culture of our organization. Figure 14.6 shows an example of the behaviors, and a scale to rate how frequently the behaviors are exhibited. The scale is the same as the one used for feedback in Chapter 12. The format leaves space for comments so that both employee and supervisor have cues to remind them of the basis of the rating.

Question: Why don't we use the behaviors in the job description for performance management?

Performance management looks at results. The behaviors in the job description are there to identify the skills needed to produce the results. They are not ends in themselves. When the supervisor and employee discuss why results were or were not achieved they use those behaviors as diagnostic tools.

"The project was successful because you questioned assumptions and identified the real problem."

"You fell below expectations on the number of customers contacted because your material was poorly organized, causing you to hunt for what you needed and take too long with each customer."

That information from rating behaviors is useful feedback for development planning.

Rating Total Performance

We can combine the quantitative and qualitative into an overall rating by weighting quantitative and qualitative results. We can weight key responsibilities at 75% of the total and behaviors at 25%. The individual key responsibilities can also be weighted, given more emphasis to some. Figure 14.7 shows the results of weighting the behaviors at 25% of the overall rating and given varying weights to the six functional areas for the administrative assistant.

Figure 14.6 Behaviors for performance management.

Exhibits the Behavior Ratings:
4 = Consistently 3 = Most of the time 2 = Some of the time 1 = Rarely

RESPECT AND VALUE COWORKERS   RATING

1. Shares information.   _____

2. Considers the potential impact of own actions on
   others and their work.   _____

3. Recognizes the contributions of others.   _____

4. Does not interrupt unnecessarily.   _____

5. Assumes responsibility for actions.   _____

6. Gives feedback when asked.   _____

7. Asks for clarification.   _____

8. Respects others' time.   _____

9. Gives others credit for ideas they originate.   _____

10. Follows through on commitments.   _____

Examples

CUSTOMER SERVICE   RATING

1. Treats internal and external customers as top
   priorities.   _____

2. Encourages and listens to customers' input.   _____

3. Acts effectively to solve customers' problems in a
   timely way.   _____

4. Is patient and understanding with external
   customers who make unreasonable demands.   _____

5. Obtains feedback from internal customers on the
   level of service.   _____

(Continued)

Figure 14.6   *(Continued)*

Examples

<small>TEAMWORK</small>   <small>RATING</small>

1. Demonstrates respect for others with diverse
    backgrounds and diverse points of view.   _____

2. Accepts responsibility for team performance, not
    just own performance.   _____

3. Helps keep the team on the task.   _____

4. Takes leadership role, at times.   _____

5. Understands how the different skills in the team
    support the team's ability to meet objectives.   _____

Examples

Overall Rating of Behaviors (If behaviors are weighted   _____
in overall performance)

Figure 14.7   Combining behaviors and key responsibilities.

Key Responsibilities	Weight	Rating	Points
1. Processes invoices.	20	___	___
2. Maintains an efficient level of supplies.	10	___	___
3. Coordinates training for staff.	10	___	___
4. Prepares statistical reports.	15	___	___
5. Prepares nonroutine correspondence and presentations.	15	___	___
6. Processes personnel data changes.	5	___	___
Behaviors	25	___	___
Overall	100		

METHOD

Weight totals 100.

Rating is based on results achieved.

Points = Weight × Rating.

Add up points and divide by 100 to get overall rating.

Overall rating _____.

▶   *To Go Further*

Fitz-enz. *Benchmarking Staff Performance.*
Mohrman, Resnick-West, and Lawler, *Designing Performance Appraisal Systems.*
Swanson, *Analysis for Improving Performance.*

See the Bibliography for citations.

Training

Setting expectations and monitoring performance are skills. Like any other skill they can be developed through training. The model for performance management includes training for both supervisors and employees. Figure 14.8 lists the modules for each.

Figure 14.8   Training for performance management.

SUPERVISOR TRAINING MODULES

▶ Developing goals for your operation.

▶ Measuring operations.

▶ Setting employee performance expectations.

▶ Coaching employees in performance management.

▶ Documenting performance.

▶ Monitoring performance.

▶ Conducting an employee meeting.

▶ Giving feedback.

▶ Giving constructive criticism.

▶ Writing results achieved.

▶ Rating performance.

▶ Avoiding rater errors.

EMPLOYEE TRAINING MODULES

▶ Measuring operations.

▶ Documenting performance.

▶ Monitoring performance.

▶ Receiving feedback.

▶ Receiving constructive criticism.

▶ Preparing a self-assessment.

Managing Performance

The model requires a concerted effort and a lot of hard work from both supervisors and employees. The payoff for the organization is that everyone is working toward the same goals. The payoff for employees is that they can see the value of their work.

Many of our organizations do not have the resources to support this model. Here are suggestions on how to obtain some of the benefits without implementing the whole model.

▶ Reduce the number of results expected for each functional responsibility. Instead of five or six, pick one.

▶ If the job description does not provide a basis for results expected, then the supervisor and employee can set them based on organizational goals.

▶ If the goals for the organization are not easy to translate to results relevant to the employee, then the supervisor and employee can set goals that have relevance to the work.

▶ Set results expected early in the year. They can and should be changed as circumstances change.

▶ Tell employees that you want their help in setting performance expectations and ask them to suggest how to do it. We do not have to follow everything they suggest but many useful ideas arise that way.

▶ If there is no formal training on how to implement performance management, then supervisors and employees can create their own methods, together.

The essentials in any implementation are:

▶ Employees know what is expected of them.

▶ Employees know how performance will be measured, how the question in the first paragraph of this chapter ("How will you and I know that the job is being performed well?") will be answered.

▶ Employees are given the opportunity to improve, based on supervisor comments throughout the year.

15

Work, Family, and Flextime

Work and Family

> "What will you do to retain me?"
> "I will help you maintain a balance between your personal and work life."

We used to work at the office, factory, or store and take care of our personal needs on our own time. Now the line between work and the personal is fuzzy. Employees work at home, do their banking at work, have flexible hours at the workplace to take care of personal needs, and bring their children to the organization's childcare facility. A lot more than work goes on in the workplace. Under the heading of "Work and Family" we:

▶ Provide personal services at the workplace.
▶ Enable employees to pursue personal interests.

Some of the practices can be classified as "nice to have." The availability of health screening at the workplace or a take-out service for meals is a convenience. Other practices such as childcare on the premises and flextime can make the difference between keeping and losing an employee. Surveys of good places to work often comment on the array of services provided.

Here are lists of popular practices:

DEPENDENT CARE

▶ Dependent care spending accounts—to help with expenses on a pretax basis.

▶ Childcare facilities—so that parents can take the children to the work site instead of having to make extra stops on the way to and from work, and can visit the children during the day (or night if that is when the parent works).

▶ Elder care assistance—referrals, subsidies, special provisions for taking care of employees' parents when they are ill or need special attention.

▶ Care of sick child—services for children who cannot go to school or usual childcare facility due to illness.

▶ Baby beepers—for husbands or friends of expectant mothers in their last weeks of pregnancy to signal when it is time to go to the hospital.

ON-SITE SERVICES

▶ Massages—a masseuse visits employees at their offices.

▶ Concierge—special services include theater and sports tickets, personal travel, and errands.

▶ Dry cleaning—vendor picks up clothes at the start of the workday and returns them by quitting time.

▶ Direct deposit of paychecks—saves the employee time and puts the money in the employee's account more quickly than the employee could himself or herself.

▶ Food—company cafeterias have been around for a long time; now they provide food that employees can take home for dinner.

▶ Travel packages—the corporate travel vendor offers vacation packages and other travel services to employees for their personal use.

▶ Miscellaneous services—automated teller machine (ATM), postage stamp machine.

▶ Fitness facilities—everything from a walking track to weights and other exercise equipment to swimming pools and saunas.

▶ Library—in addition to business materials there are how-to, general interest, hobby, fashion, and other books, periodicals, and audio- and videotapes.

FLEXIBILITY AT THE WORKPLACE

▶ Casual dress—considered family-friendly because employees do not have to spend money on a work-only wardrobe.

▶ Paid time off—replaces separate time off from work policies (such as vacation and sick leave) with a single comprehensive policy.

▶ Family and Medical Leave Act (FMLA) time off—this is a law, not a policy, but is emblematic of the flexibility in the twenty-first century workplace.

▶ Volunteer days—enable employees to volunteer services during business hours.

▶ Nonbusiness classes—aerobics, dieting, art, creative writing, karate, and other subjects.

▶ College classes—local colleges teach credit courses at our facilities during nonbusiness hours, making it easier for employees to attend.

HEALTH-RELATED SERVICES

▶ Health screening, wellness or fitness fairs—on-site health screening services such as checks of blood pressure and cholesterol identify employees at risk.

▶ Flu shots—on-site protection against the flu.

▶ Awards programs for keeping fit—employees track their participation in activities and get points toward prizes.

The Differences between the Old and New Employment Relationship

The work and family practices demonstrate how far we have moved from the old employment contract to the twenty-first century employment relationship. It was not too long ago that the fact that employees had a personal life did not matter. Organizations had standard hours and everyone complied with them. In addition to standards for hours we had standards for dress, writing style, and what you could keep on your desk or in your locker.

Employees were at work to work, not make telephone calls to check up on children or ill parents. And while employees were at their workplace they did not work out at the gym, attend a college class, or participate in a health screen for blood pressure and cholesterol. There was a dividing line between work and personal life.

To retain employees today we want to recognize and be prepared to accommodate individual differences. Work and family practices generally fall under the heading of benefits and are, as a result, available to all employees. There is another set of practices described as family-friendly that can be linked to job requirements or can be granted on an individual basis. Those practices come under the heading of flexibility in the workplace and are examined next.

A Contrast to the 1950s

The Organization Man is the title that William H. Whyte, Jr., gave to his 1956 classic book on men who belong (his term) to the organization. The book is a complex study of the relationship of work to personal values. It is clear that in the 1950s it was the corporation or institution that dominated. Employees contorted themselves and their values to conform. Today, the organization is doing the changing. It is particularly interesting to see the organization change in response to employee demands for more time for personal and family needs.

Flextime

"What will you do to retain me?"
"I will give you flexibility in when and where you work."

Perhaps the most remarkable aspect of today's workplace is the flexibility in when and where work is performed. For some organizations, work can take place at any time, in any place, and with any group of people. Giving employees flexibility while holding them accountable for results is one way to retain the people we want to keep.

Flexibility ranks high on employees' lists of what keeps them with their employer. The survey of factors influencing employees to stay or leave (see Chapter 18) showed "Flexibility in hours" in third place as an attractor, checked by 52% of respondents. "Needed more flexibility in hours of work" was a reason 9% of the respondents left their previous job.

Where Is Everyone?

At one time, if the boss looked around the workplace at 9:00 in the morning he could, literally, see all of his employees at work. Now, that same boss would see only one of 10 employees. The rest would be:

► At a customer's office.
► At a supplier's plant.
► Expected to arrive at 9:30 according to her flextime schedule.
► Working at home.
► At home, not working, because the partner in the job share is the one employee at the office.
► Working at home but planning to be at the office for a 2:30 meeting with an internal customer.
► At home, not working, because he works four 10-hour days each week and today is the day off.

Figure 15.1   Flexible work arrangements.

Flexibility can mean:

▶ *Flextime.* We establish core hours of work—for example, 10:00 A.M. to 2:00 P.M. Employees, with the agreement of their supervisors, establish regular schedules around the core. The schedules are regular so that everyone in the work group knows when their coworkers will be present.

As employers we can take advantage of this by increasing the number of hours we serve customers. If the old hours were 8:30 A.M. to 5:00 P.M., we can set new hours of 7:00 A.M. to 7:00 P.M.

▶ *Flex-schedule—four 10-hour days.* Employees work four days a week with the day off rotated so that everyone has a chance for three-day weekends.

This can increase the hours of service to customers. It also can provide continuity within a workday, if, for example, we offer one-day service.

▶ *Flex-schedule—varied by day to match the work.* If Monday and Tuesday are the busiest days of the week, the regular Monday through Friday schedule can be 10-10-8-6-6. The hours match the workload.

Employees have time on Thursday and Friday for personal use. It also may save on overtime if we have been paying it on Mondays and Tuesdays.

▶ *Telecommuting.* Employees regularly work away from the main work site and stay in touch by telephone, e-mail, and shared computer files. The regular, assigned workplace is at customers' or suppliers' facilities, on the road, or at home. Perhaps employees do not have their own work space at the organization's main site. They may have to sign up for a temporary work space when they are there.

Employees are physically closer to the customer or supplier where the "real" work takes place. Or, if the work is all by telephone or e-mail, employees can work from their homes. Call distribution systems keep them in touch with customers, and computers let them access the customer files in the organization's databases.

▶ *Working at home.* Employees work out of their home one or more days of the week. (This is done for the convenience of the employee rather than the efficiency of the work.)

What Does Flexibility Mean for Employees and for Us?

Flexibility, like other factors in the twenty-first century employment relationship, has benefits for both employees and the organization.

The ability to retain employees when their personal interests seem to collide with those of the workplace can be enhanced by:

▶ Creating leave-of-absence options to allow employees to take care of children or aged parents, going beyond the time frame of the Family and Medical Leave Act (FMLA).

▶ Accommodating employees whose spouses take jobs in other cities by allowing them to telecommute four days and commute to the office one day a week.

Figure 15.2   Sample policy on flextime.

Purpose
We provide employees with flexibility in their hours of work, on the condition that we continue to maintain superb service to our customers, both internal and external.

Policy

▶ Flextime allows employees to set work schedules to meet personal needs.

▶ Our business requirements set expectations for the presence of employees.

▶ Work schedules tell everyone—coworkers, supervisor, customers, and suppliers—when an employee is available.

▶ We have core hours of 9:30 A.M. to 3:30 P.M., when all employees are at work.

▶ Employees may ask for schedules that enable them to start work at any time between 7:00 A.M. and 9:30 A.M.

▶ Supervisors grant requests when the flextime schedule can be accommodated.

▶ Developing paid time off policies that give employees responsibility for managing their time.

▶ Listening when employees say that with the current level of electronic communications they can be as productive at home as at the office.

▶ Using the flexibility to make work time more productive.

Figure 15.1 has a list of typical flexible work arrangements along with the benefits each has for us.

Policies on Flexibility

Organizations may be attracted to the idea of being more flexible but find it hard to put into practice. Figure 15.2 shows a sample policy. Like any other policy, it has to fit the needs of the organization and be doable. Chapter 13 on work environment emphasizes the importance to retention of matching our deeds to our words.

16

Counteroffers: When We Are About to Lose Someone We Want to Retain

Picture this:

It is Monday morning; there is a knock on the door. It's Brian, your top project manager. He hands you a letter and tells you he is resigning. He has accepted an offer for a new job. The work is similar but the money is better and he will be learning new techniques. It is a shock but not a surprise. It is a shock because you are at a critical phase of a project and Brian has so far managed to keep the key client satisfied with his progress. It is not a total surprise because Brian was becoming burned out. He had asked to work on a new project that would have given him a chance to get into a new technology. You were reluctant to do it and had not looked into it yet.

Or this:

It is late on a Wednesday afternoon. You have just met with your customer service reps on the design of a new method of cutting a product's delivery time by 18%. You are especially pleased with Delores's contributions. She is relatively new to the group but already has one of the highest ratings from her customers. You ask her to stay for a few minutes. She says, "I was planning to stay because I want to tell you something. I have a job offer. I like working here but this new job would be more pay and more responsibility. I want to talk with you before I accept." You are shocked.

After you get over your surprise or shock, and panic and anxiety, you wonder if you should counteroffer.

What We Are Up Against

The conventional wisdom says the answer is "no." The reasons not to counteroffer are:

▶ *Commitment.* Brian has already made his decision. He weighed the offer and said he will accept. He has made a commitment to the other organization. See Figure 16.1 for a sample resignation letter that expresses that commitment.

▶ *Negotiating.* Delores may not really want the offer—there may be a downside to it. This may just be a negotiating tactic to get more money or a different job in our organization.

▶ *Morale.* We do not want to have a culture with the norm that the only way to get what you want is to threaten to leave.

There is also a consensus that counteroffers do not work. Even if we are successful and can get Brian or Delores to stay, it will be temporary. They are thinking about leaving and if they stay they will continue to look for another job. Our work will not get their undivided attention. We will face the same situation in another six or nine or twelve months.

Is the Conventional Wisdom Wise Today?

Are the reasons for not making a counteroffer still valid? Is it true that if we make a successful counteroffer that the employee will

Figure 16.1 Resignation letter showing commitment to new employer.

Dear _____:

Please accept this as my letter of resignation from _____.
I have accepted a new position which I believe will offer the type of
challenge, professional development, and growth potential that
will serve to advance my career both now and in the future. This
was a difficult decision to make, but I am sure you will wish me
well in my new endeavors.

I have made an irrevocable commitment to my new employer
and will be leaving my position here on Friday, _____,
2000. In the meantime, I will do whatever is necessary to make this
transition as smooth as possible.

Thank you for the opportunity to have worked with you and for
the many positive experiences I have enjoyed as an employee of

_____.

Sincerely,

_____

continue to look for another job and leave us anyway? Or, do
changes in the employment relationship suggest a different view
of counteroffers? Have counteroffers become just one more tool in
the normal, ongoing negotiation process?

In the old employment relationship there was a tacit understanding of two-way loyalty between employer and employee.
The employer was expected to continue to offer some form of re-
munerative work and the employee would expect to stay with the
employer. There was not much discussion about the conditions of
employment. In that environment a counteroffer was disruptive. It
was a way of saying that loyalty could be bought.

The twenty-first century employment contract has turned many
of the old rules upside down. Among other things, it has made
people more realistic about their business relations. The paternalistic and entitlement mentalities on the part of the employer and

employee are going away. Employees are looking at the employment contract as an exchange relationship—"what I get for what I
do." This opens the door to rethinking the old ideas about counteroffers.

Culture and Counteroffer

We can think about the employment relationship on a scale of 1 to
10 where 1 represents the old employment relationship and 10 the
twenty-first century one.

> On the scale, 1 is a benevolent society. The employer recognizes that
> he has an obligation to employees. He will do what he has to do to
> keep the organization going so that employees continue to have a
> job. Employees feel secure in that benevolence. They may or may
> not be well paid, but they feel secure. There is no need for coun-
> teroffers because employees do not consider leaving.
>
> At the other end of our scale, 10 describes an extreme free market
> organization. Employment relationships between employer and
> employees are never settled for very long. In this environment, em-
> ployers react to changes in their competitive business position by
> adjusting their skill requirements. They lay off employees with old
> skills and hire employees with the new set. They feel no obligation
> to maintain a connection with any one person. At the same time,
> employees with the desired set of skills can negotiate their own em-
> ployment packages. And, renegotiate them. Counteroffers are a
> way of life. The organizations that come closest to this model are
> professional sports teams in baseball, basketball, football, and
> hockey.

Where are you on this scale? You might want to mark where
your organization is today and where it was five years ago. It is
likely that there has been a shift upward with less benevolence
and paternalism and more free market negotiations.

Chapter 8, "Retention Starts with Selection," describes negotiations that take place when we hire a new employee. Do we continually rehire employees in the new employment relationship? If so,
then counteroffers become just one more method of doing business.

Are Basketball Teams the New Model of the Workplace?

- ► Employers make offers to and negotiate with individual employees, based on their skills.
- ► There are many ways of measuring skills: rebounds, free throws, ability to attract an audience, and so on.
- ► Each employee has an individual contract.
- ► Players are free agents and can negotiate their pay and other conditions of employment.
- ► Players move from employer to employer, even, at times, when they have a contract with the original employer.

Counteroffers in the New Employment Relationship

If we look at the employment relationship as a negotiation, then counteroffers do have a place in it. That does not mean that we use them all the time with every employee. Counteroffers are a tool to use selectively. How we use them and how frequently are related to where we are on the employment relationship continuum.

As in any negotiation, we need to know our bargaining position.

- ► *Time period.* How long do we have to retain Brian or Delores before we consider it a success?
- ► *What it will take.* We know something about Delores; after all, she has worked for us for a few months. We also have a relationship with her. We can ask her what it will take to keep her.

A Counteroffer Is Not the Same as a Retention Incentive

In a retention incentive we want to keep the employee for a defined period of time. The terms of counteroffers are variants of the current arrangement we have with the employee. They may be a salary increase, new assignment, or an extra week of vacation. It is open-ended; there is no "if-then" the way there is in an incentive.

What Happens When an Employee Leaves

A counteroffer may not make sense. The employee may be valuable but we decide we would rather replace her than make a counteroffer. We may have morale concerns about a counteroffer. We may be unable to match the offer. And, of course, we may know that there is a downsizing coming and are relieved not to have to terminate Delores's job.

Brian or Delores may not accept our counteroffer. Brian's commitment to the new employer may outweigh anything we can offer. Delores may be looking for money or opportunity that we cannot meet.

We want to remain on good terms with Brian and Delores. They probably feel the same. They know our organization and we know them. Perhaps there will be opportunities to work together in the future.

Wish Brian or Delores good luck and tell them you appreciate their contributions to your organization. You might add, "Perhaps there will be opportunities to work together in the future. We will be happy to consider your application."

IV

Putting It Together

17

Becoming an Employer of Choice

We have explored the new employment relationship, the social and economic factors affecting the workplace, and tools that we can use to retain the employees we want to keep. Now we move from the general to your unique organization. What tools can you use to improve your ability to attract and retain employees? We do this from the perspective of becoming an *employer of choice*.

Being an employer of choice gives you a competitive advantage in attracting and retaining employees. Employers of choice have distinctive qualities that influence:

▶ Potential employees to say "yes" to an offer.
▶ Current employees to stay.

Employers of Choice from the Employee's Point of View

"I want to work at a small organization; I don't want to get lost in the crowd."

"They have a great training program; I want to work there."

"They give discounts on their products; that is a great opportunity for me."

"They really help people; that's where I want to work."

"I want to be able to go home for lunch with my kids and I can do that if I work for that organization."

"I don't mind a long commute if the work is really interesting."

"They have on-site childcare; that makes a difference."

"I don't care where I work; the money makes the difference."

"They have plenty of opportunities for advancement."

"The pay isn't great but it is good for a nonprofit; so I can do something I believe in and still support my family."

Every organization can be an employer of choice. It is not a zero-sum game. One organization's success in attracting and retaining talented employees does not preclude others from being successful. There are many employers of choice, each for different reasons. One organization may be an employer of choice because of mission and technology, another because of industry, culture, and a different mission. Employers of choice compete with each other on the basis of their distinctiveness. At a time when employees are evaluating career interests, juggling work and family responsibilities, and pursuing personal growth, each organization appeals to a different part of the labor market.

Once you know what makes you an employer of choice you can:

▶ Advertise yourself to potential employees and the community at large.

▶ Remind current employees that you are a good place to work.

Gathering Data

The first step in becoming an employer of choice is to identify characteristics that make your organization attractive to employees. You may think you know what attracts and retains employees, and what works against you. Gathering data from others gives you the chance to test your assumptions. And there may be surprises.

The people with good information are:

▶ Current employees—why do they stay?

▶ New employees—why did they say yes?

▶ Former employees—why did they leave?

▶ Potential employees who turned you down—why did they say no?

Current Employees

Focus groups and surveys are two useful methods of gathering information. The survey in Chapter 18 is one starting point. You can ask employees to check all attractors and preventers. As an alternative you can ask them to rank their choices or just check the top five.

A caution: Whenever we ask employees for opinions we need to exercise care. Focus groups and especially surveys are interventions; they evoke reactions. We want to tell employees:

▶ What we are doing.

▶ Why we are doing it.

▶ What we will do with the information.

▶ That anything they say is confidential.

Chapter 20, "Employee Satisfaction Survey," describes how to conduct a survey.

New Employees

Ask new employees, even before they start, why they decided to say yes. If you regularly survey new employees to get feedback on your hiring process, you can include questions on why they decided to come to work for you. A straightforward question can produce candid information: "We are interested in knowing why you accepted our offer. Here is a list of items; check the top five. Write in anything that was important in your decision that is not on our list."

Former Employees

Exit interviews provide good information if they are carefully done. They can be conducted during the employee's last days at work or a short time after the employee leaves. The supervisor should not conduct the interview. Rather, it should be conducted by someone who is viewed as neutral. Chapter 22, "Exit Interview," has more information.

Potential Employees Who Turn Us Down

Potential employees who expressed an interest in us and then decided against us can be valuable informants. Whenever people you have interviewed subsequently withdraw from consideration or reject your offers, tell them, "We are interested in knowing why you did not accept our offer. We want to know what we can do differently to attract capable people such as you."

What Makes You an Employer of Choice

Themes will emerge as you sort out the responses. Some may be nice surprises—employees say that "Career opportunities" are an

---

Being an Employer of Choice Is a Good Thing If People Choose You for the Right Reasons

I live in the Detroit area. For years the labor market has been dominated by the automobile companies. They were employers of choice because they paid high wages, offered excellent benefits, and seemed to promise job security. (The high wages and benefits are still there but job security is less assured than in the past.) Those same factors also prevent employees from leaving. Employees, including those who wanted to change careers and try something new, find it hard to give up their pay and benefits.

---

attractor whereas you thought you were too small to provide sufficient internal movement. You may also be dismayed if few employees check "Coworkers are good" or "Sociable workplace" and you think that you have a friendly workplace.

The attractors that you want to choose to emphasize are those that are both representative of your culture and sustainable. You want to *attract* and *retain* employees. The image of yourself that you publicize to potential employees and the community has to be credible to current employees.

Advertising, Externally and Internally

Just because you have those desirable characteristics does not mean that potential employees know about them. You need to tell people. Recruiting brochures can be folders with multiple inserts for different audiences or one-page descriptions. Videos are useful for job fairs and career nights. The Web site can include one or more pages on employment opportunities as well as current job opportunities.

Recruiting material does not have to be elaborate, just clear in capturing the key characteristics of the organization. Figure 17.1 is a one-page handout that could be produced in very little time.

You also want to tell current employees why you are a good

Figure 17.1   Employer of choice handout.

XYZ Social Service Agency

We are a small organization with a big impact in the lives of the families we serve. Our customers are children who need assistance in growing into healthy adults. We provide counseling and therapeutic services as well as short- and long-term placement.

Join us and you can use your training in an atmosphere that emphasizes respect for the dignity of customers and coworkers. We support continuous learning and provide both internal and external training.

We offer a convenient location and these employee benefits:

Medical	Choose from health maintenance organizations (HMOs), preferred provider organizations (PPOs), and indemnity plans. We pay a substantial part of the premium for you and your dependents.
Dental	We pay a substantial part of the premium for you and your dependents.
Medical Spending Account	You can put aside an unlimited amount of money, pretax, to pay for HMO premiums and for medical expenses not covered by your healthcare plans.
Dependent Care Account	You can put aside up to $5000 per year, pretax, to pay for services for your dependents.
Education and Training	One week of training the first year, plus on-site seminars, satellite courses, and more.
Retirement	We offer a retirement plan that you can contribute to on a pretax basis.
Long-Term Disability	We pay the cost.
Life Insurance	We pay the cost for coverage of one times salary.
Vacation	Two weeks' paid vacation after the second year.
Holidays	Eleven paid holidays.
Childcare	On-site facility.
Internal Job Changes	We practice career opportunity; internal candidates have priority for open positions.

You will be part of a community that strives for excellence.

---

place to work. They may not recognize or appreciate what is attractive about the organization. It is easy to take some aspects of work life for granted. Share the material that you use to attract new employees with current employees. The themes can be used throughout the year in staff meetings, bulletin boards (physical and electronic), and all of the other opportunities that present themselves to remind employees why your organization is a good place to work.

)

V

Survey Research

18

Survey of Factors Influencing Employees to Stay With or Leave Their Employers

I wanted to learn more about the factors that keep employees at their current jobs and the factors that cause employees to change jobs. Many surveys on retention are from the employers' perspective. They ask employers about the issues that they believe affect retention and the programs they initiate to increase retention. I wanted to gather information on the employees' point of view.

Survey Instrument

I decided to look at four factors:

1. Reasons why employees are at their current jobs, from two perspectives:

   Attractors—reasons to stay at their current job.
   Preventers—reasons that prevent them from leaving.

2. Reasons why employees left their previous job.
3. Comparison of the current job to the previous job.
4. Employees' confidence in making a change.

In addition, there were demographic questions on:

5. Work situation:

   Type of current job.
   Industry of current job.

6. Tenure:

   Current job.
   Current employer.
   Current career.

7. Age bracket.

Results are summarized in Figures 18.1 to 18.9.

Methodology

Drafts of the questionnaire were circulated to colleagues and other volunteers. Comments on the draft survey resulted in additional items and clarifications to items, instructions, and the scale of confidence. Figure 18.10 shows the questionnaire in its final form.

Questionnaires were distributed with the assistance of colleagues and clients. I took advantage of opportunities to reach respondents who were working and attending college, both undergraduate and graduate students.

Responses

Surveys were completed by 457 respondents, all of whom were currently employed. Approximately 75% were also in school.

Not all respondents completed every question. The number of respondents in each figure is stated. All reported averages exclude missing data.

Because there were no respondents in the 65 or older age bracket it was dropped from Figures 18.8 and 18.9.

Figure 18.1   Attractors: reasons employees stay at their current job.

Respondents were given an alphabetized list of 25 items and asked to check all that applied. They were also given space to add items. Of the 457 respondents, 448 checked one item or more.
The average number of items checked, for respondents checking at least one item, was nine.
The responses in order of frequency checked are:

		RESPONSES
ITEMS	NUMBER	PERCENT
1. Benefits	257	57
2. All-around good employer	244	54
3. Flexibility in hours	234	52
4. Coworkers are good	223	50
5. Salary	212	47
6. Boss is good	206	46
7. Career opportunities	202	45
8. Challenging work	197	44
9. Work is interesting	196	44
10. Location is convenient	190	42
11. Feel needed at work	179	40
12. Skills development opportunities	160	36
13. Feel appreciated	158	35
14. Belief in the organization's mission	157	35
15. Friendships	134	30
16. Industry is interesting	132	29
17. Contribution is recognized	131	29
18. Pride in the organization	128	29
19. Sociable workplace	120	27
20. Organization is growing	107	24
21. Long-term incentives	103	23
22. Feedback is given regularly	96	21
23. Technology is state-of-the-art	83	19
24. Autonomy	67	15
25. Contractual relationship	35	8
26. Other	35	8

Figure 18.2   Preventers: reasons that prevent employees from leaving their current job.

Respondents were given an alphabetized list of 22 items and asked to check all that applied. They were also given space to add items. Of the 457 respondents, 405 checked one item or more.

The average number of items checked, for respondents checking at least one item, was three.

The responses in order of frequency checked are:

	ITEMS	RESPONSES NUMBER	PERCENT
1.	Waiting to finish my education	178	44
2.	Benefits	155	38
3.	Loyalty	97	24
4.	Do not believe I can match my pay	80	20
5.	Lose seniority	70	17
6.	Afraid to change	64	16
7.	No time to look elsewhere	64	16
8.	Do not believe I can find a job as good as mine	63	16
9.	Give up too much in incentives if I leave	61	15
10.	Unable to match my pay elsewhere	52	13
11.	Others rely on me	51	13
12.	Loss of work friendships	39	10
13.	Transportation	36	9
14.	Mentor is here	34	8
15.	Other	34	8
16.	Close to retirement	31	8
17.	Feel locked into the job	29	7
18.	Unable to find a job elsewhere	26	6
19.	Would have to relocate	25	6
20.	Close to vesting	23	6
21.	Family ties to organization	17	4
22.	Health	14	3
23.	Childcare services are not available elsewhere	10	2

Figure 18.3   Reasons why employees left their previous job.

Respondents were given an alphabetized list of 43 items and asked to check all that applied. They were also given space to add items.

Of the 457 respondents, 354 checked one item or more.

The average number of items checked, for respondents checking at least one item, was four.

The responses in order of frequency checked are:

	RESPONSES	
ITEMS	NUMBER	PERCENT
1. Lack of career opportunities	114	32
2. No opportunity to move up	101	29
3. Dead-end job	88	25
4. Was not paid what I was worth	77	22
5. Better offer of (write in)_____	73	21
6. Could not live on the pay	70	20
7. Wanted to try something different	59	17
8. Boring work	56	16
9. Unappreciated	56	16
10. Needed benefits	55	16
11. Not valued for my contribution	54	15
12. Returned to school	43	12
13. Lack of direction	39	11
14. Conflict with boss	37	10
15. Anticipated a layoff/downsizing	34	10
16. Completed college degree	34	10
17. Wanted to work full-time	32	9
18. Laid off	31	9

(Continued)

Figure 18.3   *(Continued)*

	RESPONSES	
ITEMS	NUMBER	PERCENT
19. Needed more flexibility in hours of work	31	9
20. Commute was too far	28	8
21. Didn't get resources to do the job	28	8
22. Organization did not pay for performance	28	8
23. Downsized	23	6
24. Didn't believe in the business	22	6
25. Harassed	22	6
26. Family considerations	18	5
27. No one told me how I was doing	18	5
28. Other	18	5
29. Hours were cut	17	5
30. Conflict within work group	16	5
31. Discrimination	16	5
32. Wanted to move to a different city/state	15	4
33. Had to stay at home for a while	12	3
34. Childcare arrangements were not reliable	9	3
35. Solicited by a recruiter	9	3
36. Became an independent contractor	8	2
37. Fired	7	2
38. Long-term illness or accident	7	2
39. Offered money if I left (separation)	5	1
40. Too much travel	5	1
41. Wanted to work part-time	5	1
42. Retired	4	1
43. Spouse relocated	2	1
44. Was demoted	2	1

Figure 18.4   Comparison of the current job to the previous job.

Overall, is your current job better than your last one?	
CURRENT JOB IS BETTER	**NUMBER**
Yes.	245
No.	40
About the same.	31
Not applicable; this is my first job.	19

Figure 18.5   Confidence in making a change.

How confident are you of being able to go to work at a different company and having a better work situation, whatever "better" means to you? Circle a number on the scale:

1	2	3	4	5	6
1 = Not Confident				6 = Very Confident	

The average rating was 4.7.

CONFIDENCE RATING	**NUMBER**
1 (not confident)	4
2	13
3	37
4	86
5	115
6 (very confident)	101

Figure 18.6   Work situation.

Current job:

NUMBER	CURRENT JOB CAN BEST BE DESCRIBED AS
89	Managerial/supervisory
97	Office/clerical
91	Professional/technical
44	Sales
22	Skilled/technician
36	Other
49	Checked more than one descriptor

Current industry:

NUMBER	CURRENT INDUSTRY CAN BEST BE DESCRIBED AS
29	Banking/finance
37	Durable goods manufacturing
42	Education
16	Government
40	Healthcare
16	Insurance
7	Nondurable goods manufacturing
22	Not-for-profit
23	Retail/wholesale trade
30	Services
19	Technology/telecommunications
6	Utilities/energy
29	Other
52	Checked more than one descriptor

Figure 18.7 Tenure.

Of the 457 respondents, 364 answered one or more of these items:

WORK SITUATION	AVERAGE NUMBER OF YEARS
How long have you been in your current job?	4.9
How long have you been with your current employer?	6.6
How long have you been in your current career?	9.3

Figure 18.8 Age distribution.

Of the 457 respondents, 385 replied:

AGE RANGE	NUMBER
Under 25	72
25–34	146
35–44	85
45–54	68
55–64	14

Figure 18.9 Confidence related to age.

Distribution of age and level of confidence in being able to go to work at a different company and having a better work situation for 352 of the 457 respondents who answered both items. (Scale: 1 = Not Confident, 6 = Very Confident)

CONFIDENCE LEVEL	UNDER 25	25–34	35–44	45–54	55–64	TOTAL
1	—	—	—	3	1	4
2	—	5	4	3	1	13
3	5	13	8	9	1	36
4	9	38	20	17	2	86
5	19	39	27	23	4	112
6	25	38	23	11	4	101
Total	58	133	82	66	13	352

Figure 18.10   Survey of factors that influence employees to stay with their current employers or leave.

Thank you for taking the time to complete this survey. I am doing research on retention and want to know what influences employees to stay with or leave their employers. The information you provide will help me understand the issues.

ATTRACTORS AND PREVENTERS
Let's start with your current job. What keeps you there? Usually there are *attractors*, reasons that make us want to stay, and *preventers*, reasons that prevent us from leaving. Check all that apply to you. Write in your reasons if they are not listed.

ATTRACTORS— MAKE YOU WANT TO STAY	PREVENTERS— KEEP YOU FROM LEAVING
___ All-around good employer	___ Afraid to change
___ Autonomy	___ Benefits
___ Belief in the organization's mission	___ Childcare services are not available elsewhere
___ Benefits	___ Close to retirement
___ Boss is good	___ Close to vesting
___ Career opportunities	___ Do not believe I can find a job as good as mine
___ Challenging work	___ Do not believe I can match my pay
___ Contractual relationship	
___ Contribution is recognized	___ Family ties to organization
___ Coworkers are good	___ Feel locked into the job
___ Feedback is given regularly	___ Give up too much in incentives if I leave
___ Feel appreciated	
___ Feel needed at work	___ Health
___ Flexibility in hours	___ Lose seniority
___ Friendships	___ Loss of work friendships
___ Industry is interesting	___ Loyalty
___ Location is convenient	___ Mentor is here
___ Long-term incentives	___ No time to look elsewhere
___ Organization is growing	___ Others rely on me
___ Pride in the organization	___ Transportation
___ Salary	___ Unable to find a job elsewhere
___ Skills development opportunities	___ Unable to match my pay elsewhere
___ Sociable workplace	___ Waiting to finish my education
___ Technology is state-of-the-art	___ Would have to relocate
___ Work is interesting	___ Other (write in)
___ Other (write in)	

Figure 18.10   *(Continued)*

YOUR CURRENT WORK SITUATION

JOB CAN BEST BE DESCRIBED AS
___ Managerial/supervisory
___ Office/clerical
___ Professional/technical
___ Sales
___ Skilled/technician
___ Other (write in)
_____

INDUSTRY CAN BEST BE DESCRIBED AS
___ Banking/finance
___ Durable goods manufacturing
___ Education
___ Government
___ Healthcare
___ Insurance
___ Nondurable goods manufacturing
___ Not-for-profit
___ Retail/wholesale trade
___ Services
___ Technology/telecommunications
___ Utilities/energy
___ Other (write in)
_____

RESULT OF CHANGING EMPLOYERS
Overall, is your current job better than your last one?
Yes ____   No ____   About the same ____   Not applicable; this is my first job ____

PREVIOUS JOBS
Why did you leave your last job? Check all the reasons that apply. Write in your reasons if they are not listed.

REASON FOR LEAVING
___ Anticipated a layoff/downsizing
___ Became an independent contractor
___ Better offer of (write in)
_____
___ Boring work
___ Childcare arrangements were not reliable
___ Commute was too far
___ Completed college degree

___ Conflict with boss
___ Conflict within work group
___ Could not live on the pay
___ Dead-end job
___ Didn't believe in the business
___ Didn't get resources to do the job
___ Discrimination
___ Downsized
___ Family considerations
___ Fired

(Continued)

Figure 18.10   *(Continued)*

___ Had to stay at home for a while
___ Harassed
___ Hours were cut
___ Lack of career opportunities
___ Lack of direction
___ Laid off
___ Long-term illness or accident
___ Needed benefits
___ Needed more flexibility in hours of work
___ No one told me how I was doing
___ No opportunity to move up
___ Not valued for my contribution
___ Offered money if I left (separation)

___ Organization did not pay for performance
___ Retired
___ Returned to school
___ Solicited by a recruiter
___ Spouse relocated
___ Too much travel
___ Unappreciated
___ Wanted to move to a different city/state
___ Wanted to try something different
___ Wanted to work full-time
___ Wanted to work part-time
___ Was demoted
___ Was not paid what I was worth
___ Other (write in)

_____

TENURE
How long have you been in your current job? ___ years.
How long have you been with your current employer? ___ years.
How long have you been in your current career? ___ years.

AGE
Under 25 ___   25–34 ___   35–44 ___   45–54 ___   55–64 ___   65 or older ___

CONFIDENCE IN MAKING A CHANGE
How confident are you of being able to go to work at a different company and having a better work situation, whatever "better" means to you? Circle a number on the scale:

1	2	3	4	5	6

1 = Not Confident   6 = Very Confident

COMMENTS
Please write anything else that you wish to say.

Thank you.

Respondents

The typical (modal) respondent:

▶ Checked:

Five attractors.
One preventer.
One reason for leaving the previous employer.

▶ Considered the current job better than the previous one.

▶ Circled 5 on a 6-point scale (6 the highest) on confidence in being able to go to work at a different company and having a better work situation.

▶ Checked:

Professional/technical as the current job.
Education as the current industry.

▶ Had tenure of:

One year, current job.
One year, current employer.
Three years, current career.

▶ Was between 25 and 34 years of age.

Summary of Findings

Discussions of results are included in Part III, "Managing Retention":

▶ Chapter 11, "Let's Talk about Money."

▶ Chapter 12, "Development and Career Opportunity."

▶ Chapter 13, "Work Environment."

▶ Chapter 15, "Work, Family, and Flextime."

List of Figures

VI

Other Resources

19 | *Ten Rules for Effectively Not Retaining the Employees You Want to Keep*

1. Be sure all employees are in the office every day from 8:30 to 5:00. That is when we are open for business. Just because we are on the East Coast and some of our customers are on the West Coast is no reason to come in later and stay later.

2. Do not make decisions. Ask your staff to provide more and more data. The longer you can delay making a decision, the more information you will have. Besides, the problem might go away or someone else will have the opportunity to handle it.

3. Decide to pay your employees at the middle of the market. Conduct a survey of similar companies. When results show that you are a little above the market, announce that there will be no increases this year.

4. Ask several employees to work on the same project independently. Set them up to compete with each other. When they realize that they are all trying to obtain the same material for the same reason and come to you to complain, tell them that you are only testing them.

5. Cut benefits suddenly. It is a great way to save money.

6. Do not tell employees how they are performing. After all, you are still working on their performance expectations. It is just the beginning of the second quarter.

7. Read that many of the organizations in the latest list of best places to work provide 40 or more hours of training to all employees. Announce a "Training Initiative" to provide 16 more hours of training for everyone. When you see the cost of your proposal, dump it and fire the manager of training.

8. Set up an annual incentive plan with nine goals. The payout, if all targets are met is 5% of salary. Take the first six months of the year to determine how you will measure progress. Make the first progress report at the end of the third quarter. Tell everyone, "We are behind on seven of the goals with no chance of reaching them."

9. Don't communicate the overall business plan. Let each employee work on his or her individual piece without knowing how the parts fit together. If you are the only one who knows the big picture, then you are indispensable and they are not.

10. Announce the introduction of flextime. Introduce with it a one-and-a-half-page application form in which employees have to describe why they want a different schedule and how they will be sure that the work does not suffer. Be surprised when six months later there are no employees with a flextime schedule.

20

Employee Satisfaction Survey: Taking the Measure of the Organization

How satisfied are our employees with the organization? With senior management? With supervisors? With their coworkers?

An employee satisfaction survey is one way to find out.

Here are the key steps and examples of the contents of a questionnaire.

Preliminaries

Following these three golden rules of employee surveys will make your survey a helpful and not a harmful event.

1. Do not ask about a topic unless you are prepared to respond to what you learn. It is not necessary to change something simply because employees do not like it. It is, however, necessary to tell them why we cannot or will not do so.

2. Maintain confidentiality in data collection. The people handling the raw data—collecting, processing, and reporting it—must be trusted by the entire organization. Unless you are very confident you have a person or group universally considered trustworthy, use an outside source for this purpose.

3. Maintain confidentiality in reports. If you collect demographic information, be sure that any breakdowns have a sufficient number of respondents to make it impossible to identify participants.

The working assumption here is that you have never before conducted an employee survey. Your employees have no experience, good or bad, with surveys in your organization.

There are four parts to conducting a survey:

1. Employee involvement in fostering the survey.

2. Design of the survey instrument.

3. Survey administration.

4. Management responsibility for action.

They are covered in that order, although decisions in one area affect the others.

Employee Involvement

Create a committee of employees to take responsibility for the survey. The committee may include management employees but they should not be in charge. We want employees to trust the outcome based on their representatives having a role in the design and administration of the survey. The committee may have outside help at various stages, but it will have to be the employees who:

▶ Communicate to the organization.

▶ Decide what topics to cover.

► Design or approve questions.

► Determine how data will be collected, processed, and reported.

Decide if the whole process can be conducted by employees or if you need outside assistance for specific assignments.
Create interest in the survey prior to its distribution.

► Tell employees that it is coming and when.

► Tell employees why you are doing it.

► Tell employees how they will hear about the results.

► Emphasize confidentiality.

Tell employees the results.

► Distribute high-level results—for example, the scores on each question, average for each dimension, and general themes from open-ended questions.

► Ask supervisors to discuss results with their staff.

► Have senior management tell employees what they are doing with the results.

Design of the Survey Instrument

Determine the dimensions that are important to employee satisfaction in your organization. Overall employee satisfaction is derived from satisfaction with various dimensions of the work environment. These differ from organization to organization. Typical dimensions are:

► Benefits.

► Career opportunities.

► Communication—organizational.

► Compensation.

▶ Coworker support.

▶ Diversity (internal).

▶ Diversity (with respect to treatment of customers).

▶ Fairness.

▶ Flexibility.

▶ Organizational communications.

▶ Pride in the organization.

▶ Recognition and rewards.

▶ Respect.

▶ Safety.

▶ Supervision—overall.

▶ Supervisor communications.

▶ Supervisor fairness.

▶ Supervisor support.

▶ Teamwork.

▶ Training and development.

▶ Trust.

Two methods of identifying the dimensions that are useful for your organization are:

1. Combing and sifting through recommendations from management, issues emerging from your open-door policy, and topics raised in employee publications.
2. Testing a wide range of possible dimensions to determine which are the best predicters of overall employee satisfaction.

Develop three or four questions for each dimension. Questions should:

▶ Be pertinent to the dimension.

▶ Have a single point.

See Figure 20.1 for examples of questions that are good and not good.

Use three or four questions to get at each dimension. It is desirable to test the questions prior to conducting the survey to make sure that:

▶ They are clear to the employees who have not been involved in preparing the questions.

Figure 20.1 Guidelines for questions.

1. One topic per question.
2. Questions relate to dimension.
3. No reverse questions (e.g., "We treat people badly").

Here are examples of questions on "supervisor communications" dimension:

Good: "I have the information I need to do my job."

Good: "My supervisor keeps me informed about changes at our organization."

Not good: "I depend on my supervisor for information about changes in the workplace such as new technology and new products." (Mixed content; the employee may agree on new technology and disagree on new products.)

Not good: "I have the information I need to make decisions about my benefits." (Not pertinent to dimension; supervisor is not the main source of information about benefits.)

Not good: "I do not have enough information on factors affecting my work." (Phrased negatively; all questions on each dimension should be interpreted similarly on a chosen scale.)

▶ All of the questions associated with a dimension are interpreted similarly.

Decide how many questions to ask. If you pretest the survey that process will give you your answer. Otherwise keep the number of questions within a range of 30 to 50. You want enough questions to gather valid information on all of the dimensions that are most important to employee satisfaction in our organization. At the same time you want a good response rate and lengthy surveys may appear burdensome.

Develop a scale—see Figure 20.2 for examples.

Decide if you will use open-ended questions. They give employees an opportunity to speak their minds about issues that are not covered in the survey or that they want to tell you more about. They do add to the cost of the survey because they have to be transcribed and analyzed. See Figure 20.3 for examples of open-ended questions.

Decide if you will collect demographic data such as age, gender, ethnicity, or work unit.

Figure 20.2   Examples of rating scales.

Alternative 1: Employees interpret questions for themselves and use a continuum scale of 1 to 7 where:

1 = Strongly disagree and 7 = Strongly agree.

Alternative 2: Anchor the scale and avoid a middle ground:

1 = Strongly disagree.

2 = Disagree.

3 = Agree.

4 = Strongly agree.

Figure 20.3 Examples of open-ended questions.

What do you like best about our organization?

What is your opinion of your work environment?

How well do you think senior management has performed in responding to changes that affect our organization?

How well do you understand our strategy?

What can you personally do to increase employee satisfaction in our organization?

No survey can cover all aspects of employee satisfaction. Please use the space below for any additional comments.

▶ Reason for: to identify issues relevant to particular groups.

▶ Reasons against: may inhibit responses and cut down on the number of employees participating.

Survey Administration

Determine the format. At one time surveys were done with pencil and paper, requiring someone to transcribe and key in the responses. Now we have alternatives, based on the technology available to us. See Figure 20.4 for those methods.

Decide what to include in the survey package. You may wish to distribute:

▶ Memo from the survey committee encouraging employees to participate.

▶ Memo from the chief executive encouraging employees to participate and emphasizing the importance of the information to the organization.

▶ Instructions on completing the survey and where to send it.

Figure 20.4   Methods of preparing surveys.

For rating scale:

▶ Paper questionnaire, employee responses are keyed in.

▶ Paper questionnaire, employee responses are scanned in.

▶ On-line questionnaire, employee keys in own data.

▶ Paper questionnaire, employees respond by telephone to a voice response unit.

For open-ended questions:

▶ Handwritten.

▶ Typed and scanned.

▶ E-mailed to outside vendor.

▶ Statement of how employees will learn the results.

▶ Statement of confidentiality.

Management Responsibility

The response from senior management determines how employees view the process. Is it seen as a real desire by management to find methods of improving employee satisfaction? Or is it a charade? For it to be the former, members of the management team should:

▶ Tell employees their own reaction to the results.

▶ Give employees an overview of plans of action that deal with specific issues.

▶ Tell them what management will not be taking action on, and why.

Strengthening the Survey Process

There are statistical techniques that refine the value and improve the usefulness of a survey. You may wish to have someone within your organization with experience in surveys and the trust of employees join the survey committee. If you use an outside consultant, choose one who can provide this service.

21

Employee Handbook

The desirability of designing and communicating policies was described in Chapter 13 on work environment. Here are directions on how to produce an employee handbook for that purpose.

Preliminaries

Before starting on the handbook decide on the desired legal relationship with employees. Legal relationships include at will, for cause, satisfaction, and personal employment contract. Whatever we choose has ramifications for other policies affecting the work environment.

There are software programs and books with sample policies and procedures. We can borrow handbooks from other organizations or go on-line and read some. They can give us ideas of what to include in our own employee handbook. However, each organization is unique. Culture and legal environment are different from organization to organization. Each organization's handbook has to reflect its individuality and cannot be a copy of another organization's. Employee handbooks should be reviewed by legal counsel.

Writing Style

The way policies are written is as important as what they say. Style sets the tone of the relationship between management and employee. We can be inclusive or prescriptive. Here are statements from two different organizations on attendance guidelines:

> We believe that we all want to contribute to the organization's success. Our ability to compete is based, in part, on the continuity of services we provide to our customers. We know that coworkers count on us to be at work for our scheduled time, and our salaries are based on that expectation. We realize, therefore, that regular attendance is necessary in order for our business to operate efficiently and without costly interruptions.

> Employees are expected to be at their desks and ready to work at their scheduled start times. All absences, except emergencies, must be approved by a supervisor prior to the scheduled start time.

Style also refers to the choice of pronouns. We can write policies from one of three perspectives. For example, a policy on "Hours of Work" may be:

- ▶ Impersonal: "The workweek begins on Sunday at 12:01 A.M. and concludes at midnight the following Saturday."
- ▶ Management to employee: "Your workweek begins on Sunday at 12:01 A.M. and concludes at midnight the following Saturday."
- ▶ Inclusive: "Our workweek begins on Sunday at 12:01 A.M. and concludes at midnight the following Saturday."

Accessibility and Accuracy

Employee handbooks are living documents. The contents change in response to internal changes in our organization and external changes in the legal and regulatory environment. The days of hardbound handbooks kept in the supervisor's office are gone. We want every employee to have easy access to the latest information. Two methods are:

▶ Loose-leaf binders, with each page dated and updated from time to time.

▶ On-line, provided that all employees have reasonable access through computers either at their own desks and workstations or at kiosks.

Contents

Any or all of the following may be included in an employee handbook. Figure 21.1 is a table of contents for an employee handbook of policies.

▶ Policies.

▶ Procedures, including forms.

▶ Supervisor's manual for employees who have to interpret and implement policies.

▶ Employee benefits and services.

▶ New employee orientation.

Follow-Up

There are two audiences that we want to reach:

▶ *Employees.* Whenever we distribute a new handbook we want to:
Give employees an overview of the contents.
Have employees sign a statement that acknowledges receipt of the handbook. The statement is kept in their personnel files.

▶ *Supervisors.* We want them to have a supervisor's manual and training on how to interpret any policies that they have to implement.

Figure 21.1   Table of contents of an employee handbook.

LETTER FROM THE CHIEF EXECUTIVE

ACKNOWLEDGMENT OF RECEIPT OF HANDBOOK
Once signed by the employee the receipt goes in the personnel file.

EMPLOYMENT RELATIONSHIP

At will
For cause
Satisfaction
Personal employment contract

INTRODUCTION AND WELCOME

History
Mission statement
Vision statement
Organizational or functional structure
Diversity statement
Equal Employment Opportunity (EEO) statement

OUR WORK ENVIRONMENT

Behavior on the job
Business ethics
Individual responsibility
Personal privacy
Work area privacy
Harassment
Drug and alcohol abuse
Smoking
Dress
Computer software usage
E-mail

Figure 21.1 *(Continued)*

Internet and telephone usage
Safety
Confidentiality
Lobbying
Use of organization's assets
Retaliation

EMPLOYMENT

Job classification
Employment classification
Overtime
Employee records
Filling positions
Immigration law compliance
Employment of relatives
References

COMPENSATION, RECOGNITION, AND EXPENSES

Compensation philosophy
Salary administration
Performance evaluation
Performance counseling
Recognition
Suggestion system
Travel and business expenses

OPPORTUNITIES

Development philosophy
Educational assistance
Educational programs
Training
Career responsibility

(Continued)

Figure 21.1   *(Continued)*

FACILITIES

Practical information about work facilities
Maps and driving directions
Transportation and parking
Location of our facilities and nearby places of interest
Company identification card
Access to our facility
On-site services

ATTENDANCE (EXPECTATIONS ABOUT BEING AT WORK)

Work schedule
Attendance
Notification of absence
Vacations
Holidays

LEAVES OF ABSENCE

Sick leave/personal days/paid time off
Leave without pay
Military leave of absence
Jury duty
Bereavement
Return to work
Family and Medical Leave Act

TERMINATION OF EMPLOYMENT

Voluntary resignation
Discharge
Reduction in force
Severance pay
Exit interviews
Job abandonment

Figure 21.1   *(Continued)*

CONDUCT AT WORK

Problem resolution

Standards of conduct

Conflicts of interest

HEALTH AND WELLNESS

Wellness programs

Health facilities

22

Exit Interview

One way we can learn employees' opinions of our organization is to ask them as they leave. Our hope is that they will tell us what they really think because they are no longer part of our organization and have nothing to lose by being honest.

Preliminaries

Our hope for good information from former employees may be dashed because they:

▶ Are concerned about references.

▶ Want to leave open the possibility of working for us in the future.

▶ Are naturally polite.

▶ Do not care sufficiently to tell us anything useful.

▶ Have a real issue that they are wary of discussing.

The last reason may include some form of discrimination or harassment. If there are any concerns that an employee may be leaving because of such an issue we need to follow up both for the good of our workforce and for legal protection. Consider conducting follow-up exit interviews for a period of time. Contact employees three months after they leave. Using open-ended questions, ask about their reflections on their working experience. An outside agency with interviewers trained to probe responses may identify issues that were initially hidden.

Conducting the Interview

Alternative methods of conducting exit interviews include:

1. Human resources conducts the interview during the last few days of employment while covering benefits and other topics. This is best done early in the last week but not the last day of employment, which is often crowded with a good-bye lunch or packing or finishing up work.
2. Human resources or an outside service conducts a telephone interview a week after the employee leaves.
3. An outside service conducts a telephone interview three months after the employee leaves.

There are pluses and minuses to each approach. Waiting puts the experience in perspective. On the other hand, once employees leave they may be uninterested in responding to our questions.

Interview Format

Figure 22.1 is an example of an exit interview. It shows three question formats:

▶ Use of a rating scale—easy to score and analyze.

▶ Short answer—can explain what is behind the ratings.

▶ Open-ended—has the potential for gathering better information.

Figure 22.1 Exit interview survey.

We want to know your opinion on work life at our organization. Please rate the items using this scale:

1	2	3	4

1 = Disagree   4 = Agree

In our organization:

___ My work was challenging.

___ I received the training I needed.

___ My contributions were recognized.

___ Benefits were good.

___ Communication within the organization was open.

___ I received good cooperation from other departments.

___ My work unit functioned as a team.

___ I had sufficient flexibility in my hours of work.

___ Methods used to determine salary increases made sense to me.

___ I had good potential for career growth.

___ I was able to obtain the resources I needed.

___ My salary was competitive.

___ I had the autonomy I needed to do my work.

___ I was able to find a reasonable balance between my work and my family needs.

One of the good things about our organization that I will miss in my new position is:

_____.

One thing I will be glad to leave behind me is:

_____.

(Continued)

Figure 22.1   *(Continued)*

Comments (additional information):

_____

_____

_____

_____

Here are statements about your supervisor. Respond using the same 4-point scale.

1	2	3	4

1 = Disagree   4 = Agree

My supervisor:

___ Demonstrated fair and equal treatment.

___ Showed commitment to our organization's mission.

___ Provided recognition on the job.

___ Developed cooperation and teamwork.

___ Encouraged and listened to suggestions.

___ Resolved complaints and problems.

___ Followed policies and practices.

___ Provided regular feedback on my performance.

___ Treated me fairly.

___ Discussed my career goals with me.

___ Gave me useful feedback regularly.

What did you like most about your supervisor? _____

_____

_____

Figure 22.1   *(Continued)*

What did you like least about your supervisor? _____

_____

_____

What prompted you to seek alternative employment? _____

_____

_____

What is better about your new job and new organization? _____

_____

_____

Closing question:

Would you recommend us to a friend as a place to work? Why or why not? _____

_____

_____

Follow-Up

Many organizations do a good job of collecting exit interview data, but they may not always summarize and analyze it. This is a rich source of data in our goal of retaining the employees we want to keep. If we do not know why they leave us, we are unable to take steps to keep them. The "retention czar" mentioned in Chapter 4, "As We Go Forward," should be sure that someone is designated to follow up on this information.

Special Issues

If we learn anything that refers to illegalities such as embezzlement, inappropriate conduct such as harassment, or unsafe working conditions, it must be investigated. We can try to get the employee's permission to cite him or her as a source. If unable to do so, we can attempt to get specific information that will help in an investigation. Even if it appears that the source is an unhappy employee trying to make trouble, we have an obligation to follow up and turn the information over to the appropriate parties in our organization.

Bibliography

Books and Articles

Block, Peter. *Stewardship: Choosing Service over Self-Interest.* San Francisco: Berrett-Koehler, 1993. Describes a model of redistributing power from the supervisor to all members of the team and organization.

Boyatzis, Richard E. *The Competent Manager: A Model for Effective Performance.* New York: John Wiley & Sons, 1982. Identifies competencies (skills) and behaviors related to successful managerial performance.

Cascio, Wayne F. *Costing Human Resources: The Financial Impact of Behavior in Organizations.* Boston: PWS-KENT, 1991. Details methods of measuring the benefits as well as the expenses of human resources programs such as employee assistance programs and selection techniques.

Chingos, Peter T., ed. *Paying for Performance: A Guide to Compensation Management.* New York: John Wiley & Sons, 1997. Examines how compensation affects organizational goals.

Davis, Brian L., et al. *Successful Manager's Handbook: Development Suggestions for Today's Managers.* Minneapolis: Personnel Decisions International, 1996. Gives ideas of how supervisors can develop their staff members.

Deems, Richard S. *Hiring: More Than a Gut Feeling.* Franklin Lakes, NJ: Career Press, 1995. Presents practical approaches to conducting behavioral interviews.

Douglas, James A., Daniel E. Feld, and Nancy Asquith. *Employment Testing Manual.* Boston: Warren, Gorham & Lamont, 1989 plus updates. Covers, in detail, issues related to employment testing. With annual updates.

Fay, Charles H., and Howard W. Risher, eds. *New Strategies for Public Pay: Rethinking Government Compensation Programs.* San Francisco: Jossey-Bass, 1997. Takes compensation practices in the business sector and applies them to government units.

Fitz-enz, Jac. *Benchmarking Staff Performance: How Staff Departments Can Enhance Their Value to the Customer.* San Francisco: Jossey-Bass, 1993. Uses benchmarking as a method of linking organizational goals to functions and teams.

Flannery, Thomas P., David A. Hofrichter, and Paul E. Platten. *People, Performance, & Pay: Dynamic Compensation for Changing Organizations.* New York: The Free Press, 1996. Describes four types of work cultures and explains how to align pay with each.

Gubman, Edward L. *The Talent Solution: Aligning Strategy and People to Achieve Extraordinary Results.* New York: McGraw-Hill, 1998. Describes how to manage people who give the organization a competitive advantage.

Gupta, Nina, and Jason D. Shaw. "Let the Evidence Speak: Financial Incentives *Are* Effective." *Compensation & Benefits Review,* March–April 1998, pp. 26, 28–30. One side of a discussion on money and motivation. See Kohn, "Challenging Behaviorist Dogma" for the other.

Hamel, Gary, and C. K. Prahalad. *Competing for the Future.* Boston: Harvard Business School Press, 1994. Explains how organizations can create their own futures.

Herman, Roger E. *Keeping Good People: Strategies for Solving the Dilemma of the Decade.* Greensboro, NC: Oakhill Press, 1997. Provides a primer for starting to think about retention.

Janz, Tom, Lowell Hellervik, and David C. Gilmore. *Behavior Descriptive Interviewing: New, Accurate, Cost Effective.* Englewood Cliffs, NJ: Prentice Hall, 1986. Describes the background and how-to's of behavioral interviewing.

Judy, Richard W., and Carol D'Amico. *Workforce 2020: Work and Workers in the 21st Century.* Indianapolis: Hudson Institute, 1997. Projects workforce demographics.

Kanter, Rosabeth Moss, and Barry A. Stein, eds. *Life in Organizations: Workplaces As People Experience Them.* New York: Basic Books, 1979. Describes how people are affected by and react to the work environment.

Kohn, Alfie. "Challenging Behaviorist Dogma: Myths about Money and Motivation." *Compensation & Benefits Review,* March–April 1998, pp. 27, 33–37. One side of a discussion on money and motivation. See Gupta and Shaw for the other.

———. *Punished by Rewards: The Trouble with Gold Stars, Incentive Plan$, A's, Praise, and Other Bribes.* Boston: Houghton Mifflin, 1993. Asserts that rewards do not motivate and are usually counterproductive.

Lawler, Edward E., III. *Strategic Pay.* San Francisco: Jossey-Bass, 1990. Describes how to develop compensation programs that support strategy.

McAdams, Jerry L. *The Reward Plan Advantage: A Manager's Guide to Improving Business Performance through People.* San Francisco: Jossey-Bass, 1996. Links individual employee performance to organizational success.

MacDonald, Cameron L., and Carmen Sirianni, eds. *Working in the Service Society.* Philadelphia: Temple University Press, 1996. Describes work environment issues facing employees in the service sector.

Mohrman, Allan M., Jr., Susan M. Resnick-West, and Edward E. Lawler III. *Designing Performance Appraisal Systems: Aligning Appraisals and Organizational Realities.* San Francisco: Jossey-Bass, 1989. Guides planning and implementing performance appraisals.

Nelson, Bob. *1001 Ways to Reward Employees.* New York: Workman Publishing, 1994. Lists ideas for appreciation and cash awards for all types of reasons.

Peter, Laurence J., and Raymond Hull. *The Peter Principle.* New York: William Morrow, 1969. Describes how employees move through organizations.

Peters, Thomas J., and Robert Waterman. *In Search of Excellence: Lessons from America's Best Run Companies.* New York: Harper & Row, 1982. Tells principles of management of successful companies.

Pfeffer, Jeffrey. *The Human Equation: Building Profits by Putting People First.* Boston: Harvard Business School Press, 1998. Makes the case that organizational success depends on people.

Schuster, Jay R., and Patricia K. Zingheim. *The New Pay: Linking Employee and Organizational Performance.* New York: Lexington Books, 1992. Suggests how to link total pay to the organization's performance.

Smart, Bradford D. *The Smart Interviewer.* New York: John Wiley & Sons, 1989. Shows techniques for interviewing and selection.

Spencer, Lyle M., Jr., and Signe M. Spencer. *Competence at Work: Models for Superior Performance.* New York: John Wiley & Sons, 1993. Links competencies to identifying the right person for the job.

Swanson, Richard A. *Analysis for Improving Performance: Tools for Diagnosing Organizations & Documenting Workplace Expertise.* San Francisco: Berrett-Koehler, 1994. Connects employee training and development to the organization's business requirements.

Thornton, George C., III. *Assessment Centers in Human Resource Management.* Reading, MA: Addison-Wesley, 1992. Describes, comprehensively, assessment centers and their role in managing human resources.

Ulrich, David, and Dale Lake. *Organizational Capability: Competing from the Inside Out.* New York: John Wiley & Sons, 1990. Describes techniques of management practices to build success based on people.

Waterman, Robert H., Jr., Judith A. Waterman and Betsy A. Collard. "Toward a Career Resilient Workforce." *Harvard Business Review,* July-August 1994. Describes the attitudes and actions of employees who take responsibility for their own careers.

Whyte, William H., Jr. *The Organization Man.* New York: Doubleday, 1957. Describes the experience of a middle manager in the 1950s.

Wilson, Thomas B. *Innovative Reward Systems for the Changing Workplace.* New York: McGraw-Hill, 1995. Describes methods of rewards for today's organization.

Yukl, Gary A. *Leadership in Organizations.* Englewood Cliffs, NJ: Prentice Hall, 1981. Surveys theories and practices of leadership.

Resources

Professional Organizations

These are the major professional organizations for the topics covered in this book. Although they are membership organizations, many of their resources are available to nonmembers. The web sites have good information as well as links to other useful sites.

American Compensation Association
14040 N. Northsight Boulevard
Scottsdale, AZ 85260
(602) 922-2020
www.acaonline.org
Compensation and benefits.

American Society for Training and Development
1640 King Street
Alexandria, VA 22313-2043
(703) 683-8100
www.astd.org
Training and development, including technical training.

Employee Benefits Research Institute
Suite 600
2121 K Street, NW
Washington, DC 20037-1896
(202) 659-0670
www.ebri.org

Benefits in depth, including work and family topics.

Society for Human Resources Management
1800 Duke Street
Alexandria, VA 22314
(800) 283-7476
www.shrm.org

All topics in human resource management. The Employment Management Association, which focuses on staffing, is a professional emphasis group (PEG) within SHRM.

Surveys on Retention, Rewards, and the Work Environment

Aon Consulting. *America@Work 1998: A Focus on Benefits and Compensation.*
———. *America@Work 1998: The 1998 Workforce Commitment Index.*
———. *America@Work 1998: An Overview of Employee Commitment in America.* 1998. These examine employees' commitment to their employer in the new employment relationship.
Interim Services, Inc. *The Emerging Workforce.* 1998. Examines the values, expectations, and experiences of employees in the new workplace.
Manchester, Inc. *Retention & Staffing Report: Trends and Analysis.* 1998. Retention methods and turnover by organizational levels and industry.
Saratoga Institute. *Retention Management: Strategies, Practices, Trends.* 1997. Strategies organizations are using to affect retention.
Society for Human Resources Management. *1997 Retention Practices Mini-Survey.* 1997. Issues related to retention and the initiatives organizations take in response.

Watson Wyatt. *Strategic Rewards.* 1997. Strategies employers are using to retain employees.

Periodicals

The preceding professional organizations have useful publications. In addition:

Compensation & Benefits Review
American Management Association
(800) 262-9699
www.amanet.org/periodicals/cbr

Fast Company
(800) 688-1545
www.fastcompany.com

Fortune
(800) 621-8000
www.fortune.com

Harvard Business Review
(800) 274-3214
www.hbsp.harvard.edu

Workforce Magazine
(800) 444-6485
www.workforceonline.com

Index